Miller writes with cand[...]
of both experience and[...]
every leader in the church and every follower of Christ. Equal parts
handbook for what to do when sexual abuse happens and narrative for
how to empathize with and care for victims of sexual abuse, *Healing
Together* is a must-read.

LORE FERGUSON WILBERT, AUTHOR OF *HANDLE WITH
CARE* (2020)

Healing Together casts a compelling vision for the support of sexual
assault survivors. It is a practical guide and first-aid resource written
with the wisdom, honesty, and understanding of a survivor. This book
explains clearly the effects of trauma, which is vital to our response and
care for survivors. We will assign it in seminary courses we teach on
preventing, recognizing, and responding to abuse.

JUSTIN S. HOLCOMB AND LINDSEY A. HOLCOMB,
AUTHORS OF *RID OF MY DISGRACE* AND *IS IT MY
FAULT?* JUSTIN IS A BOARD MEMBER OF GRACE.

This is the most well-rounded book on abuse I've read to date. It is the
perfect balance of personal narrative, spiritual implications, medical
definitions, and practical application. This is an invaluable resource.
Thank you for telling your story and sharing your expertise, Anne!

JIMMY HINTON, PASTOR, ADVOCATE, HOST OF *THE
SPEAKING OUT ON SEX ABUSE PODCAST*

Anne Miller has penned a forthright narrative of how a pastor sexually
abused her as a kid and how the Southern Baptist Convention betrayed
her when she reported it. Thankfully, she doesn't offer up platitudes
for such traumas, but rather, in this "bandage of a book," she simply
seeks to "help people help survivors." And in that sort of heart-sourced
help, there is hope.

CHRISTA BROWN, AUTHOR OF *THIS LITTLE LIGHT*

An incredibly practical book on how to love the broken in our midst. This is a love letter to the church, asking her to rise up, put on empathy's shoes, and weep alongside the weeping. Miller's heart for others, her spot-on typification of trauma, and her love for Jesus emanate from these help-filled pages. Highly recommended.

MARY DEMUTH, AUTHOR OF *WE TOO*

Rarely do you read a book from someone who is a survivor of sexual assault, a gifted writer, a student of trauma and abuse, and an advocate for other survivors. But Anne Marie is all of those. She uncovers the relatively hidden world of sexual trauma that only we survivors and trauma therapists see. Remarkably, she has distilled complex concepts and made them straight-forward without over-simplifying. This is a stand-alone achievement.

MIKE PHILLIPS, COAUTHOR OF *OVERCOMING PORN*

Pastors, friends, and family members of survivors, if you have a desire to understand the heart of a survivor and know the many different phases of grief we experience, *Healing Together* will open your eyes to the ugliness of clergy abuse and how it affects the heart and life of a survivor years later.

Survivors will find themselves agreeing with many of the emotions that are evident in the pages of this book as Miller walks through her journey.

Raw, heart-wrenching, and eye-opening, Miller's story grabbed my attention, and many times, I found myself sobbing. While I remain an active member of a Southern Baptist church, this book is a knowledge-able read and worth your time, whether you are a believer, Southern Baptist, survivor, or have a desire to learn more.

MEGAN NICHOLS LIVELY, SBC ADVOCATE AND SURVIVOR

Healing Together

A Guide to Supporting Sexual Abuse Survivors

ANNE MARIE MILLER

ZONDERVAN
REFLECTIVE

ZONDERVAN REFLECTIVE

Healing Together

Copyright © 2019 by Anne Marie Miller

Requests for information should be addressed to:
Zondervan, *3900 Sparks Dr. SE, Grand Rapids, Michigan 49546*

ISBN 978-0-310-11208-2 (softcover)
ISBN 978-0-310-11212-9 (audio)
ISBN 978-0310-11209-9 (ebook)

Scripture quotations are taken from The Holy Bible, New International Version®, NIV®. Copyright © 1973, 1978, 1984, 2011 by Biblica, Inc.® Used by permission of Zondervan. All rights reserved worldwide. www.Zondervan.com. The "NIV" and "New International Version" are trademarks registered in the United States Patent and Trademark Office by Biblica, Inc.®

Scripture quotations marked CSB® are taken from the Christian Standard Bible®, Copyright © 2017 by Holman Bible Publishers. Used by permission. Christian Standard Bible®, and CSB®, are federally registered trademarks of Holman Bible Publishers.

This book is a source of information only and is intended to supplement, not replace, the advice of a trained professional. The resources identified are accurate as of the date published. The author and the publisher expressly disclaim responsibility for any adverse effects arising from the use or application of the information contained herein.

Any internet addresses (websites, blogs, etc.) and telephone numbers in this book are offered as a resource. They are not intended in any way to be or imply an endorsement by Zondervan, nor does Zondervan vouch for the content of these sites and numbers for the life of this book.

Cover design: Studio Nth, LLC
Cover photo: © Stas Malyarevsky/Shutterstock
Interior design: Emily Ghattas

Printed in the United States of America

19 20 21 22 23 / LSC / 10 9 8 7 6 5 4 3 2 1

To Charlotte
I don't understand how God found me worthy enough to
be your mom, but it's the greatest privilege in the world,
and my greatest joy. You're the most amazing girl I know.
Your hugs are epic. I love you, monster. Beep, beep.

Don't participate in the fruitless works of darkness, but instead expose them.

EPHESIANS 5:11 CSB

LORD my God, I called to you for help,
    and you healed me.

PSALM 30:2

Carry one another's burdens; in this way you will fulfill the law of Christ.

GALATIANS 6:2 CSB

Contents

Author's Note

To supporters and loved ones of sexual abuse survivors—Healing Together is not an easy read. It is full of words and acts that we have been told never to speak about, especially in church. For far too long, we have looked the other way, whether it be out of discomfort, shame, fear, or survival.

You will be uncomfortable reading this book. You should be. Abuse should make us uncomfortable, sad, and angry. If you need to put it down for a moment, take a deep breath, and go for a walk, please do. But pick it up again. We must stare these evils in the face and confront them as we walk alongside survivors who have endured them. The reason sexual abuse has continued to perpetuate in modern society is because for too long many people have not been willing to stand under the immense weight and grief and evil that it causes. It isn't easy, but it's necessary, now more than ever.

But if you find yourself becoming overwhelmed to the point of *despair* while you read this book, please reach out for help. Talking to a trusted friend, counselor, or leader is key as you process this. We don't need to be perfect to help someone, but we do need to be healthy. Do not sacrifice your own physical, emotional, mental, or spiritual health as you take this on. I recommend you read this book as a group so that you can process the difficult truths you find and can converse openly about how it affects you. In Galatians 6:2, we learn we should carry each other's burdens, and processing the content of this book with those in your trusted community is one of the ways you can do just that.

Dearest survivors—this book is written for you too, as many supporters are also survivors, but many words, stories, and details may "trigger" or "activate" your trauma, potentially inflicting additional suffering. Please know your boundaries before reading this book. If you're unsure, ask those close to you whether they think it's wise for you to read it in this current season of your life.

This book is not meant to be gratuitous or shocking, but because of the nature of its contents, you will likely be disturbed. These things aren't very "Christian" to talk about, and that's kind of the point. They are evil. And it's time to confront that evil so that, as the title says, we can begin healing together.

Preface

When someone you love shares that they were sexually abused, do you know how to respond? The Me Too movement (#MeToo)—large numbers of women and men coming forward and sharing their own experiences of sexual abuse, assault, or harassment—has permeated our conversations all around the world, both online and in person, and it isn't losing momentum.

Survivors of abuse in the church have found the courage and space to speak out too. Offshoots of #MeToo were born, indicating and disclosing abuse in everything from schools to Hollywood, from restaurants to, yes, religion. The #ChurchToo movement has become broadly used to describe any abuse within a church environment. Denominational and organizational movements within #ChurchToo have popped up as well, telling the stories of those who have been harmed in all sorts of Christian groups, non-profits, and mission agencies. In recent years, megachurch pastors have been surrounded by sex scandals, and seminary presidents have been fired for covering up rape. Church volunteers working with children have been caught red-handed for committing abuse acts at their church. And with almost every week that passes, it seems as if a different pastor or church leader has been fired, has resigned, or has been arrested for sexual misconduct. The abuse is widespread. In March 2019, Cardinal George Pell, the highest ranking official in the Catholic Church, was convicted and sentenced to six years in prison for sexual abuse, the culmination of decades of revelations of abuse within the Catholic Church. And many Protestant churches and organizations are realizing that they too need to examine their structures, policies, and ways of preventing abuse as they are forced to deal with their own scandals.

In fall 2018 a Baptist university in Texas asked me to speak to their student body about my story of being sexually abused in my teens by a Southern Baptist seminary student and youth pastor. The university I spoke at didn't want to shy away from the #MeToo or #ChurchToo conversation. They wanted to help their students and to give them a place to share their stories and come forward if they needed help.

After my talk, some of the faculty approached me, asking me what they should do if one of their students came forward. They couldn't find any resources to help guide and support someone who had been abused or to equip those walking alongside them. They were familiar with textbooks discussing theories and the biology and history and sociology and psychology of abuse, but they didn't know how to respond if a student said to them, "I was sexually abused. I need help. What do I do?" Answering this question can be complicated, and there is no simple, step-by-step guide for answering it in a way that will fit every situation. To help them, I suggested some books and organizations to look up, but I admit, I felt helpless in my answer.

A few days later, as I was performing the mundane task of washing out our garbage can, it hit me. It was one of those very rare moments when I could almost audibly hear the voice of God speaking to me, saying, "Write something that can help people help survivors." It was clear, and I knew it could not be ignored. Still, I argued back, "But I'm not an author anymore. I gave up that career. You don't understand. I'm in nursing school, and that requires *math*. I work at a hospital helping high-risk pregnant women. I have a preschool "threenager" who is constantly being saved from death-defying moments a hundred times a day and throwing tantrums because her green beans are green. I'm exhausted. No way. You've got the wrong girl."

The back and forth raged on, as our wrestling with the Spirit always does, but I knew God wasn't going to let up. I learned a long time ago that arguing with God is a waste of time. So with mixed emotions of resignation and gratefulness, I walked back into the house and told my husband I knew exactly what I needed to do: write a guide outlining the basics of how to help someone who has suffered the trauma of sexual abuse.

As I looked around for similar resources, I became even more convinced that there is a massive need for a resource developed for the *average person* out there—the mom or dad, aunt or niece, teammate or roommate, the butcher or baker or candlestick maker—who wants to support a loved one who has survived sexual abuse. We can't leave the responsibility for care to the professionals or even the church because a lot of survivors won't reach out to a counselor or step back into a church. We need something to help the typical friend or family member understand what abuse is and how to support someone who has gone through it. And while there are some resources available, many of them are difficult to find or require a PhD in clinical psychology to understand them. So if you never quite finished that thesis on neurotransmitters and behavioral therapy, I've written this book for you.

Before we continue, this preface is intended to let you know a couple of things.

First, I want to introduce myself. I'm a survivor of childhood clergy sexual abuse and a perpetual student of understanding the science behind trauma and evidence-based approaches to healing it, especially within a faith-based context.

You should know that I am not an expert psychologist or a doctor. Frankly, I'm a burned-out evangelical author and speaker who quit writing a couple of years ago (it's okay to laugh here). What I am an expert in is trying and failing and giving up and hoping and trying again. This book is case in point.

I grew up Southern Baptist, but it's been a few years since I have found a church home. I think this is an important disclosure. After a *Houston Chronicle* article was released (documenting over seven hundred cases of sexual abuse within the SBC),[1] I was interviewed on NPR's *Morning Edition* by Rachel Martin. She asked me about my current thoughts on church attendance. As I told her, I admittedly miss church, but currently, I am too fearful to return, for my own health as well as the safety of my daughter. In the interview I said I love Jesus and I believe in the work he's done on the cross for us all, but to quote myself, "It breaks my heart to know that there are men and women who have destroyed other men and women and children under the name of Jesus, and in God's name and in God's house."[2] In other words, "church" is something I'm still working on.

Professionally, I'm in nursing school with the goal of one day serving as an advanced practitioner working with sexual abuse victims (either in forensics as a Sexual Assault Nurse Examiner [SANE] or in psychiatry as a pediatric Psychiatric Mental Health Nurse Practitioner [PMHNP]). Even though I don't work directly in mental health at my hospital, many of our clinic's patients have multiple mental health issues, and some are survivors of abuse, incest, and trafficking. I volunteer in a local group for mothers seeking advice to better support their daughters with depression, anxiety, OCD, and eating disorders. I should be (fingers crossed) passing my boards, finishing certifications in my specialties, obtaining my graduate degree and advanced practitioner licensing within the next three to five years, respectively. #PrayForMe.

Second, there are a couple of things I want to make clear before you begin.

This is not an in-depth study or theological exploration of common cultural issues of the day such as gender, authoritarianism, patriarchy, purity culture, law and order (*dah-dum*),* or history. This is a basic guide to help people walk with survivors of sexual abuse or misconduct. It's a foundational building block to get you started. It's written with Christian undertones because that's a part of my story—both my abuse (I was sexually assaulted and abused by a Baptist seminary student and pastor) and my healing (I've been in the Christian world for almost forty years, but I feel as if I'm still quite new to this faith thing in a personal sense).

I mention some organizations and people by name, including some within the Southern Baptist Convention. This is not an attempt to tear down this denomination, harm the church, or

---

* Not calling *you* a dah-dum, but if you've ever seen *Law and Order*, you know what I'm saying.

bring shame on people. Jesus does not need us to uphold his reputation. We should not care what "the world" will think about "the church" when abuse is revealed. Instead, we should care about what *Christ* thinks about abuse in his church. Hiding abuse is hypocritical. Bringing it to light is not. The Bible instructs us to expose evil deeds of darkness instead of hiding or participating in them (Ephesians 5:11).

Now that you know what this book is not, here's what it is: *this book is meant to be first aid.* Please know there is a long recovery process ahead that's going to require a team of people in multiple disciplines, such as counselors, therapists, doctors, pastors, friends, family members, support groups, etc. If finding expert voices such as these is at the top of your priority list, or if you are a pastor looking for a training experience to require of all your staff members on handling cases of abuse, you can go to the Godly Response to Abuse in the Christian Environment (GRACE)'s website—netgrace.org—and click on "Books" to learn more.

And the last thing: a legal disclaimer.

This book is meant to be first aid.

Even though it is on public record, for the sake of this book and for posterity, I refer to the man who abused me by only his first name, Mark. When I write or speak about my abuse, the major events and the timeline are disclosed accurately. But in this book, any dialogue, including names of other people and additional irrelevant details, are edited, condensed, paraphrased, or are a composite of various conversations. It's important to note that no situation or experience in this book has been exaggerated or sensationalized, but the names of other people and some details of other stories have been changed or composited to protect the survivors and to maintain the integrity of any ongoing investigations and criminal proceedings.

As the church wrestles with what to do and how best to lead through seemingly never-ending headlines about sexual abuse, survivors can't wait. Before we bleed out, we need help applying pressure to the wounds of sexual abuse. So to help you better understand the delicate dynamics of abuse and to walk alongside survivors, I offer you this bandage of a book. Writing is the best way I know to help, and I hope that together we can start healing.

Thank you for your patience and grace as you jump into this book with me. I truly believe the title, *Healing Together*, clarifies what we *all* need. I know I could not have made it this far in my life without many, many other people who have cried and listened and walked the path alongside me. I believe that by helping a survivor of sexual abuse, you will be enriched and encouraged too. Together we can become whole and healed (James 5:16). I'm praying for each person who will read this book and for each person who is suffering with the horror of abuse. It's time for us to walk together, hand in hand, to face the evil that wants to destroy us.

> Before we bleed out, we need help applying pressure to the wounds of sexual abuse.

Chapter 1

My Story of Childhood Clergy Sexual Abuse

I grew up in the church as the daughter of a Southern Baptist pastor.

My mother, my father, and my grandpa attended Southwestern Baptist Theological Seminary (SWBTS). My dad and grandpa were ordained pastors in small, rural Texas towns. My parents met at SWBTS as they worked toward earning their master of divinity (MDiv) degrees. My mom was salutatorian in her MDiv class of 1977 and was one of the first women to graduate with that degree. After an Easter play at Retta Baptist Church in 1984, I understood why Jesus died for me. My father baptized me when I was five years old at a small church in the Texas Panhandle.

When I was growing up, church was my second home. With all its flaws and fundamentalism, it still felt safe to me. There wasn't anything atypical about my childhood other than the fact that we moved every couple of years to small towns all over west Texas. For a Southern Baptist pastor, this was the normal life of ministry.

When I was sixteen years old, two weeks into my junior year of high school, my family moved from west Texas to the Dallas area after my father resigned from the last church he would ever pastor. My new high school was huge, and the culture of the large city shocked me. It wasn't easy to make friends, and there were no obvious Christian organizations on campus. One afternoon I went through the parking lot and put copies of a homemade flyer on every car as an invitation to a Bible study before school— but nobody showed up. In a last-ditch attempt to make friends, I chose to lead a See You at the Pole event at my school. Since we were new to town and my family hadn't found a church yet, I went online to find a youth pastor who could help me gather some materials to promote the event. Maybe there was a pastor out there who knew some other kids in town who would want to come. Maybe he'd have experience at other See You at the Pole events and could give me ideas about getting people to show up.

It was 1996, and because most churches didn't have websites yet, the only way I knew to look for someone was to use America Online's (AOL) profile search feature. After scanning through several profiles, I found a pastor who was attending SWBTS, the same seminary my parents had attended. And he lived in Arlington, where I lived. Win-win. His name was Mark. I emailed him, told him I was a junior at a local high school, and I asked whether he could help me get some posters and flyers to advertise See You at the Pole. He emailed back and said he could help. We arranged to meet at a McDonald's in the food court at Hypermart, a superstore close to my house.

My mom drove me, and together we met Mark. They exchanged pleasantries and connected over their shared background in ministry. After the meet and greet, she stepped away for a few moments to grab some groceries while Mark and I continued talking at McDonald's.

There was nothing remarkable about Mark's appearance. He wore khaki cargo shorts, a polo shirt, and a baseball hat (though I could tell he was bald underneath). I guessed he was in his midtwenties. He had kind blue eyes and a few inches on my five-feet-seven frame.

Mark asked about me, about my school, and about the move to Dallas. I was encouraged that someone seemed to care about me and might want to be my friend. Mark helped me gather the materials I needed to promote the See You at the Pole event, and then we wandered through the store and found my mom. They talked a bit more about seminary, which professors were still there, and what classes Mark was taking. My mom found out that he served as a missionary with the same organization she had served with twenty-five years earlier, and they swapped a few more stories as our groceries traveled up a sticky black conveyer belt to the Hypermart cashier.

We paid and left.

There were no red flags flying. No warning signs that my life, my innocence, my faith, and my future would soon be bulldozed by trauma. All signs said *you can trust this guy.* He is in seminary— the same seminary your parents attended. And he cares about students in the area. And he's been a missionary.

After See You at the Pole, Mark contacted me to ask how it went. As with the Bible studies I had tried to start, nobody had showed up, further cementing my sense that God didn't care about

> *There were no warning signs that my life, my innocence, my faith, and my future would soon be bulldozed by trauma.*

my life. I was now a month into my new school, and I had next to no friends.

I told Mark about my disappointment with God. At my last school, I hadn't been the most popular kid, but I had been involved in sports and honors society and several of the Christian clubs. As a preacher's kid, I was expected to do everything at church, so I kept a busy schedule. Leading people and serving people fulfilled me. I felt as though I had been faithful to God—so why was he punishing me?

"Maybe I should just quit," I complained.

"Quit what? School?" Mark replied.

"Quit faith. Quit God. None of this makes sense. If there even were a God, I'd be better off without him."

"Don't do that, Anne," he said. "Can you come over? Let's get something to eat, and we'll talk about this."

—

I told my parents I was headed out, and they gave me a time to be home, as they always did. As a sixteen-year-old in the nineties, I never thought that a quick visit with the local youth pastor was something I needed to spell out or ask special permission to do, and they trusted me. I was the quintessential good preacher's kid.

Mark lived on the north side of Arlington, but the drive from where we lived on the south side wasn't too bad. I remember feeling slightly uncomfortable in the rundown area of town where his apartment complex was located, but I saw him standing in the breezeway of his building, silhouetted by the hallway light. I parked my mom's car in one of the few empty spaces. His building was in the very back of the complex, and my mom's car faced a dilapidated wooden fence. I walked up to the breezeway where Mark was standing.

He invited me inside his apartment. The kitchen light was on, and the apartment was so small that it provided enough light for the living room and the adjacent small dining area. The TV was also on, casting a bluish tint to everything.

"I thought we could have some pizza," he said, pulling a box from the freezer. "Do you want to go get some ice cream too?" he asked, opening and closing his refrigerator and freezer doors.

Of course I wanted ice cream. We got into his car—a nineties blue Pontiac Grand Am—and drove to a grocery store about five minutes away. Whatever flavor he chose wasn't one I wanted, so I got chocolate, my favorite. He paid for our ice cream, and we left, driving right back to his apartment.

"Is that your car?" His car lights shone on my mom's silver Chevy Lumina as he turned into the parking lot by his apartment.

"Nope. It's my mom's. I just started working after school, so I hope to buy my own car pretty soon. Riding the bus to school isn't the greatest. I don't know what I'd get, but I know my dream car—a turquoise Camaro—is out of the question for now."

He parked the car next to a yellow Ford Ranger truck.

"Not that you're asking my opinion," he said, "but I think girls who drive yellow trucks are hot."

"I like trucks too," I said, unsure of how to respond.

"My couch is kind of uncomfortable," he said, tilting his head in the direction of the couch as we walked through the door. Mark got two spoons from the kitchen and opened the ice cream. We sat on the floor, eating the ice cream, along with some pizza, with the TV on in the background. I learned a little bit about his family, where he grew up, and how he had just returned from being overseas.

He asked whether I wanted to watch a movie, and I said yes while returning the pints of ice cream to the freezer. Blankets from his couch were already on the floor, and we sat underneath them, with some movie flickering in front of us. The pizza, the ice cream, the movie, and the laughs—this felt familiar. It felt like the stuff of typical teen youth group hangouts—which I knew well as a pastor's kid. Finally, I felt a little more at home in this new town. For the first time in weeks, I felt happy. Someone wanted to spend time with me.

Mark shifted under the blanket, and his shoulder grazed mine and then softly pressed against it so that our arms were touching. His hand found mine and he held it. My heart suddenly raced with fear and anxiety. Wait . . . was he *interested* in me? But I was a student. In high school. I froze and waited for the credits to roll.

It was late when the movie ended, and I had school the next day.

"I should probably go." I stood up. "Do I owe you anything for the ice cream?"

"Don't worry about it," he said. "You can buy it next time."

I thanked him for having me over. "I miss hanging out with my old youth pastor and his wife. This was nice."

Mark walked me out to the breezeway, and we hugged goodbye. He stood there by his apartment door and watched me walk to my mom's car. I turned, waved, got in, and drove home, telling myself that maybe I was overthinking things. Maybe I was anxious for no reason. Maybe he was just trying to be nice.

At this point, I did not understand the part that isolation and confusion play in sexual abuse. I had experienced an initial wave of anxiety when Mark made his first move toward me, brushing up against my shoulder and holding my hand. But I stifled the red flags going off in my head because I had an equally strong wave of feeling seen, understood, and valued. I was a vulnerable teenager who finally found a person (whom my parents and I assumed was trustworthy), and he thought I was worth being friends with. No sixteen-year-old should have to know that seeking out someone who is isolated, drawing them in, and then confusing them are common abuse strategies. That's what was happening to me, and I was clueless.

When I got home, my mom, a primary school teacher,* looked up from the couch where she was grading papers. "Did you have a good time?"

"I did," I said naively. "I think I'm finally starting to make some friends."

—

Mark and I continued spending time together over the next three months, mostly at his apartment. Then, between Thanksgiving and New Year's, he suddenly stopped responding to my emails and phone calls. I saw him on AOL's Instant Messenger one evening and sent him a message asking what had happened. He

---

* So much for putting that MDiv to work. She has never regretted earning it, but finding a position in a church where she could actually use it was a challenge she tried unsuccessfully to overcome.

said he was out of town for the holidays with family and would be back once school started up again. Sure enough, when the spring semester started back up, so did our encounters.

I suppose there are certain red flags that you see as clear as day in adulthood that you just don't as a teen. Other than that first trip to get ice cream, there were only two times in six months that we ventured outside Mark's apartment. Once, we went to a restaurant in downtown Fort Worth about thirty minutes away from where he lived. I got food poisoning there and will never forget the ride home. He drove my mom's car and went the wrong way on a one-way on-ramp. I was terrified that we'd be hit before he could turn around, and the velocity of the quick U-turn he did pushed me against the passenger door so hard I was afraid I would throw up all over the place. Being sixteen, I also thought it was a hilarious adventure and remember that I couldn't stop giggling.

The only other time we went out in public was when we visited Greenbriar Park, near the seminary in Fort Worth. Greenbriar Park is located near where my grandparents live, and every time I visited them, I would drive by the park. As I wrote this book, I found myself driving by Greenbriar Park several times a week. My grandma was diagnosed with lung cancer the summer before I started writing this book, and our family would visit her as often as we could. She passed away on May 7, 2019. Every trip we took to see her carried a shadow of my abuse, a testament to the power of trauma. (For more information on trauma, see appendix A.) Even something as sacred as my grandmother's final months of life has threads from my past abuse woven into each visit.

As a pastor's kid in the south, I was naive and conservative, not to mention terrified of sex. I understood sex as one of the worst "sins" (outside of murder) one could commit. My parents never talked to me about sex, and while I knew the anatomy and physiology of how it all worked from health class, that was it. Before I met Mark, I had a couple of "boyfriends," guys I would "go out" with, but nothing was ever serious. I had held hands with boys and had even shared a few awkward kisses. A boy from my junior high Sunday school class and I were caught kissing behind the church one Sunday morning, and I thought I would die when people found out. Another time, a (different) boy who attended one of our youth evangelism events tried kissing me on an indoor roller coaster in Mr. Gatti's, a cheap pizza arcade,* but I thought it was gross and shoved him away. I was committed to saving sex for marriage and proudly wore my gold purity ring—that my dad had purchased from a Sears catalog—as a freshman in high school.

As Mark and I spent more time together, the sexual component of the relationship escalated significantly. Holding hands turned into kissing, kissing turned into passionate kissing, and that led to even more intimate activity, both above and below the waist. I can recall one moment with such clarity that I can tell you exactly what I was wearing and where in his apartment we were lying on the floor. This, I believe, is when my mind disassociated from reality—when the trauma of what I was experiencing had the most impact.

I was wearing a green shirt and jeans, and Mark and I were making out on the floor between the right side of the television and the kitchen. He was on top of me, then rolled off to the side in between the TV and me, and propped his head up on his

---

* How did any of us survive the 1990s?

hand, elbow on the floor. I was still on my back. I turned my head toward him.

"Are you a virgin?" he asked. The question stunned me a bit. Other than telling my best friend about the few boys who had kissed me, I never talked to anyone about sexual stuff, and nobody had ever asked me about my virginity.

"Yes? . . ." I stammered. In my best good-girl Baptist voice, I added, "You know, because true love waits. I don't believe in having sex until you're married."

"Oh, right . . . right," he said emphatically. "I believe that too."

Unsure of what to say next, I awkwardly asked, "Are you?"

"Well, no," he responded. "I lost my virginity when I was thirteen. Even though I was a Christian, I wasn't really walking with God then, and it was a huge mistake. I'm waiting for marriage now."

Thirteen? That seems so young . . . His words struck me then, and I've never forgotten that conversation—or what happened after it.

Mark climbed back on top of me and continued kissing me, but then he took it further. I felt as though I couldn't tell him to stop. I was frozen. Terrified. Paralyzed. I couldn't say no. I couldn't say yes. I couldn't say anything. I didn't want to do what we were doing, but I also didn't want to lose his friendship, his attention, or the affection I thought he had for me. Now, after time spent in counseling, I know this was the moment when my body and my mind broke what I was experiencing into separate pieces so I wouldn't be mentally or emotionally present as Mark guided our hands and bodies beyond my comfort and beyond my experience.

One day in April Mark suddenly ended our "relationship." It

was unusual for us to spend time together during the daytime—another red flag I can now see so clearly in hindsight—so I must've been skipping school, or perhaps it was a weekend.

What I distinctly recall is that he asked whether I remembered him talking about a female friend of his. I did. Once when I was at his apartment, she had called and he picked up. She was an overseas missionary he had met right before he came back to the States. He took the call in a room with the door closed, but I didn't think anything of it at the time.

Mark told me she was returning to the US, and they planned on getting married in *December*—only eight months away. He had to end all contact with me and could never see me again. He told me she could never know about it.

I was confused, shaken, and overwhelmingly heartbroken. We never talked about our relationship status, but I thought Mark and I were dating—in a relationship—exclusively. Why else would we have a physical relationship? Why else were we spending all this time together? Had he been cheating on me with this woman the whole time? Or wait—was he cheating on her with me while she was overseas? Was I the other woman? It eventually became clear that he had used me, an isolated sixteen-year-old girl, simply for his sexual pleasure. He didn't care. And now that he couldn't continue using me, I was cast aside, thrown away, discarded. I felt like garbage, and like an idiot for not seeing this "relationship" for what it was.

I've never been good at asserting myself, so I doubt I made a scene. I don't remember what happened next. My next memory is me, sitting in the back seat of my mom's car, the following day. We were at a gas station, and I was pretending to be sick to my stomach, lying down in the back seat while my younger brother rode shotgun. Curled up and facing the back of the car, I penned a poem in my school notebook.

Part of it reads:

> *Inside the night sky lay a mystery*
> *sweetened with curiosity and the thrill of risk.*
> *You close your eyes, reach up toward the sky,*
> *bring down your hand a bloody fist.*
> *It tells a tale of forgotten love,*
> *a whisper wind so peaceful trusting, true.*
> *But the sugarcoated stars tell lies,*
> *they never reveal truth to empty hollow eyes.*

I felt guilty from the "sin" of what had happened. To my sixteen-year-old self, it felt as though Mark "broke up" with me. What I didn't understand at the time was that a youth pastor (or any adult outside of family for that matter) should never have kept a teenage girl inside his apartment, isolated and out of public. And more than that, he should never have been *physically on top of me.* I was impressionable and spellbound by what I thought was—and *what he made seem to be*—genuine love. I was blinded by the exhilaration of having *a man* of God interested in me, an overlooked and lonely *girl.* In the culture in which I was raised, the role of pastor was the most honored of roles, and to be the woman chosen to walk alongside a pastor was something most of my female peers aspired to. In my mind, I was following in the footsteps of my grandmother and my mother, both pastors' wives. I had believed that God had redeemed his absence in my life by sending Mark to me and trusting me in this sacred role.

In the aftermath of his disappearance, I was horribly depressed. I missed lots of school. My parents didn't know this because a friend who worked in the attendance office made sure the phone tree never called my house to inform my parents that I was absent. I went from an A+ student to a B student in one semester. Eventually, I made Cs in several classes and barely passed my English class. I spent most of my time in bed, under my pink and white polka dot bedspread. My parents knew I wasn't myself, but they assumed I was still sad from moving and having to leave behind all my friends. I was really, really good at hiding.

> I was blinded by the exhilaration of having a man of God interested in me, an overlooked and lonely girl.

I graduated from high school right after my seventeenth birthday. I opted not to go to college, a major change of plans. A prestigious university had offered me a scholarship when I was in eighth grade, because of my test scores. But now I didn't see the point of attending college and instead went to work full-time. I moved out of my parent's house into my own apartment. That summer, I started casually dating someone—we'll call him John—who became a family friend (and remains so even now). As we swapped stories of prior unrequited loves, the only thing I could think to tell him was that my previous "boyfriend" was a seminary student who had broken up with me because he was with—and got engaged to—someone else throughout the entirety of our relationship. John was infuriated. He wanted to know Mark's name, but I wouldn't tell him. I was afraid he would find him and say or do something to him if I told him. I just wanted to forget about it all.

A few months later in December, I found myself wondering whether what Mark had told me about getting married was actually true. I searched for his wife's name on AOL, and sure enough, there was her screen name. Mark's username was still active too, and through that, I found their missionary website. There were many times over the next couple of years when I wanted to email his wife to tell her what had happened, but I didn't want this innocent woman to have her heart broken by Mark too.

I didn't yet understand that my past "boyfriend" experience was actually *abuse*. But as I entered my twenties, I started to realize that the significant age difference between Mark and me was disturbing. I began referring to him as the "creepy youth pastor" when conversations about past relationships came up. I was beginning to recognize that something was wrong, deeply wrong, about the dynamics of our relationship, but when it would cross my mind, I was careful to stuff it right back into the category of "things I don't want to think about." I stayed busy to distract myself.

Life continued. I started working in a church, rediscovering my faith in God. I even got married. From time to time, I had nightmares and flashbacks of the abuse, and when my husband would touch me in certain ways, I would have panic attacks or completely freeze up. Having sex usually hurt—badly—but I had no idea why. I went to a gynecologist who specialized in sexual disorders. She examined me and told me there was nothing physically wrong with me.

I walked out of her office feeling completely broken.

Recognizing My Abuse

In the summer of 2005 I worked at a church and volunteered in student ministry. One of the male interns on the student ministry team, Josh, was my age—turning twenty-five, and a girl I was mentoring, Millie, sat next to me at his birthday party at the church. She was sixteen. I looked at Josh on stage, talking about how embarrassed he was because he thought twenty-five was so old. I looked at Millie with her glittery fingernail polish and algebra books tucked under the table.

Wait. Mark was a twenty-five-year-old pastor. I was a sixteen-year-old student. That would be like Josh dating—and being intimate with—Millie. I felt sick to my stomach. The significance of the age difference smashed into me, and I saw how inappropriate it was for any adult (an adult pastor, at that) to have a sexual relationship with such a young girl. The thought hovered over me like a shadow as I went home and went to bed.

The next day, still reflecting on the Josh/Millie theory, I was straightening up my house. *Oprah* was on the TV in the background. Oprah was talking about sexual abuse, and someone on the show was explaining how a predator groomed his victims.[1] He said something about how kids who recently moved to a new area were the easiest targets. They didn't know anyone. The predator would find out different things they liked and what they were interested in. He would give them attention, listen to their problems, and earn their trust. Once he felt they were comfortable with him, he'd introduce something sexual into the conversation—like a joke—and see how they responded. If they didn't push back, that's when he would start engaging in sexual activity, slowly and strategically, always taking it a step further each time. When he got bored or it got too risky, he'd stop.

I was shaking. I went to the bathroom and splashed cold water on my face. What this man on *Oprah* said mirrored my experience with Mark. At twenty-five, this was the first time I realized that what had happened to me wasn't a romantic relationship that simply "ended."

What had happened to me was *abuse*.

It wasn't just sin.

It was a *crime*.

I went to a counselor at my church. Quietly, I told her, "I think I may have been sexually . . . abused." Saying the word *abuse* out loud, labeling my identity as a victim, shattered me. The counselor confirmed that what had happened to me was undeniably sexual abuse, and we looked Mark up on the internet. We found that he was serving as a missionary for a Christian organization. At the top of the website there was a photo of Mark, his wife, and their three children, with a biography of the family written underneath it.

The counselor told me that because so much time had passed, and because he was in such a high position of leadership in his organization, it was likely that what had happened was a one-time thing and he probably had accountability now. She believed it would do more harm than good to investigate it any further and urged me to focus on forgiving him for what he had done so that I could move on.

That's what I did for the next year. A little over a year later, at the suggestion of my counselor, I wrote Mark a letter letting him know that what he had done was wrong, that I was hurt by it, and that I forgave him. It was brief and factual. I sent it to the email address listed under his family's picture on his missionary website. Because the email address was just their last name, I didn't know whether it was a family email address or his personal one. Just in case his wife read the email before he did, I added a postscript for her, something to the effect of: *If you are reading this and this is the first time you've heard about me or this relationship, I'm so sorry.*

I never received a reply to the email.

"Finally," I thought, "maybe this is over."

The Next Level

Shortly after sending the email, I was asked to write an article on forgiveness for my church's magazine. Because it was still fresh in my mind, I used the experience of forgiving Mark for sexually abusing me as the example for the article. I generically mentioned in the introduction that I had been sexually abused in high school and focused most of the article on my process of forgiveness. After it was published, the daughter of one of our pastors came to me and told me she had a similar experience of abuse. She asked where Mark was now, and I told her he was a missionary, and I named the organization he worked with. At the time, I didn't know that her dad also worked closely with that organization in his pastoral role at our church.

She ended up telling her dad that "hypothetically" a missionary with this organization had sexually abused a girl a decade ago when the man was twenty-five and the girl was sixteen. Her dad asked her if the man was currently in ministry, and she affirmed he was. At that point, he told her to "cut the hypothetical" and to tell him what she knew. Not wanting to betray my trust, she came to me the next day and explained what she had shared with her father.

The fact that Mark was in ministry and the idea that he could be abusing other children or teens still haunted me. I saw this as an opportunity to find out once and for all whether I was the only person this had happened to, and as a way of making sure other kids were safe. I agreed to meet with my friend's father, and I agreed to let him contact Mark's organization.

The organization responded quickly and asked me to relay all the details of my abuse that I could remember. They confronted Mark with the accusation, and Mark denied it. I was shocked. How could he just deny it? I had been certain he'd confess when he was confronted with the truth.

The organization conducted a thorough internal investigation to determine whether my accusation was credible and warranted further action. Over the course of two months—September and October 2007—they questioned me, my family, Mark, his family, and various friends. For two full days they asked for every detail—every intimate detail—that I could remember. They asked whether I was sexually active before Mark, or after him. How "far" had I gone with other boyfriends? Was there anything I did to entice Mark? They contacted the man I dated after Mark, and asked him how I dressed, suggesting that I perhaps was responsible for leading him on or tempting him. Their approach to this investigation—especially the unmistakable overtone that I was the one who did something wrong—retraumatized me. I became even more depressed, anxious, and suicidal after they were done.

A few months after they finished their investigation, they concluded that my accusation was credible and backed up by evidence and the testimony of people they interviewed. They said Mark had a sexually inappropriate relationship with me, that I was suffering and traumatized from it, and that Mark lied to them about the nature and extent of our relationship.

During their investigation, the organization asked whether I intended to press charges against Mark. Because of the overwhelming emotional pain directly following their investigation, I told them I did not anticipate pressing charges. I did not think I could walk through the process of answering all those questions again. And because they didn't ask me if I wanted them to report it or not, I thought they surely had to report it.

In early 2008 I received an email from the organization's general counsel that said Mark was no longer employed by them and that he didn't appeal their conclusion. I took this to mean he had been terminated for his actions toward me. And once again I found myself thinking, "Finally, this is over."

No Penalty Box

A few months later, I learned that Mark was now a pastor at a Southern Baptist church in Arkansas.

What? How?

It didn't make sense to me that a man who was credibly accused and determined to have sexually abused a teen by an organization affiliated the Southern Baptist Convention could go on to pastor within that same denomination. My mind tried to make sense of it. *Maybe he did end up confessing. Maybe he abused only me. Maybe he is in some kind of "restoration" plan back into ministry.* This was the only logical answer I could think of. It didn't sit right with me, but I trusted these ministry leaders. It was in my blood to trust them. Something this big couldn't fly under the radar. They had to know, and somehow, it had to be okay. They told me it was over and to move on, so I tried.

Except I couldn't.

A couple of years later, I was driving and I saw a midnineties blue Grand Am—the type of car Mark drove when I knew him—and I had to pull over because I felt as though I couldn't breathe. This led me to look him up again, to see whether there was any other news out there about his abusive behavior.* I found that he was still a pastor but at a different, larger church in Arkansas. I noticed that even though each staff member listed first and last names on their website biographies, Mark went by only his first name. Was he trying to hide? Was he trying to make it harder for people to find him? I set up a Google Alert on his name so that any time his name was published online, I'd get a notification. I told myself that if anyone else came forward or if he was arrested, I'd come forward. I was scared to do it alone; I wanted to know whether others were out there, harmed the way I had been. Maybe if others could be strong, I could be too.

I never addressed the trauma from the abuse or from the Christian organization's response and investigation. I didn't know I needed to. I chalked all the anxiety, depression, and fear of sexual intimacy up to genetics and a religious upbringing. But

---

* One of the symptoms for Complex Post-traumatic Stress Disorder, which I was diagnosed with in 2010, is to frequently look up or give attention to the person who is responsible for the trauma. In various therapies, I've learned that this is a self-protection mechanism. If I know the "threat" is far away from me, my body can relax a bit. https://www.bridgestorecovery.com/post-traumatic-stress-disorder/complex-ptsd-symptoms-behavior-and-treatment/.

everything came to a head in late 2010, when I wrote a book called *Permission to Speak Freely.* In that book I shared the story of my abuse—broad enough not to identify anyone but detailed enough so people knew what happened—and my recovery. I went on a book tour to support its release, and on an almost weekly basis, I would talk about my mental health and how healing from the abuse was an ongoing process. I thought this experience would be empowering, or perhaps a way to finally deal with it all, but it turned into a formula for emotional disaster.

Maybe if others could be strong, I could be too.

In late 2010, at the tail end of the tour, I found myself thinking about suicide again. I did not see a reason for living after this book tour was done. I told a friend, and his family intervened and helped me check into a residential trauma treatment facility in Arizona, where I finally began to see how the abuse affected me. I spent an entire month working through an intensive healing process, and before I left, my mentor in the program asked me a question that reflected my own unanswered question—how, after what he did, could Mark still pastor at an SBC church?

On February 13, 2011, at 11:47 p.m., I emailed my contact at the Christian organization my question:

> How can Mark still pastor inside SBC churches like he is? (Any church, really, but SBC in particular?) Isn't (sic) there some checks and balances with something as serious as what he was terminated for?
>
> I'm not going to "go after" him again—It's taken me this

long to deal with that initially . . . I know where he works and that he hides his last name on the website and every time I pass through Little Rock I'm terrified of seeing him . . .

But my mentor had a really legit question I thought. So I said I would ask. If you can't disclose that, I fully understand.

As with my email to Mark in 2006, I never got an answer.

The Next Right Step

For the next several years, I remained in counseling, and after a season of healing, I continued to write and speak. My husband, Tim, and I got pregnant, and in July 2016 our daughter was born. The abuse remained a part of my story, but I felt that I had been healed from the trauma.

Right before our daughter was born, my fifth book, *5 Things Every Parent Needs to Know about Their Kids and Sex*, was published. After that book released, I "retired" from writing and speaking in order to stay home with her and to start nursing school. But in the spring of 2018, I was asked by some friends to speak at their church in California. They wanted me to help lead parents to having healthy conversations with their kids about sex. As I prepared my talk, I reflected on my past. Every time I had told my story from a stage in the past, someone would ask me, *What happened to the guy who abused you?* I would say he was terminated from his job within the denomination, but he's still a pastor at one of their churches. It never made sense to those I shared this with, and it never made any sense to me.

Legally, I was under the impression that the statute of

limitations (the amount of time the law allows for criminal charges to be brought against someone—it varies from state to state) had passed for pressing criminal charges. I had even written that in 5 *Things*! But as I talked to two of my friends about this upcoming event at the church, one of them sent me a link to an article about a girl who was sexually assaulted by her youth pastor in Texas when she was seventeen years old. Apparently, there is *no* statute of limitations for sex crimes involving minors in Texas. Did that mean Mark could face criminal charges after all? I combed through the legalese of the penal code online and tried to make sense of it all.*

The article mentioned an attorney in the Dallas–Fort Worth area who worked on child sexual abuse cases involving churches, so I emailed him, and we spoke for a while. Yes, he told me, Mark could face criminal charges, but there was more to my call than I had expected. The attorney was a mandatory reporter—meaning he was legally obligated to report any crime such as this. And now that he knew about it, and even though this wasn't the reason I had contacted him, one of us had to report Mark. He gave me the option to do it, and he informed me that if I didn't, he would.

I said I would report what had happened, and I followed through as soon as I got off the phone with him. Since my abuse had happened twenty-two years before this phone call, I didn't expect to hear anything from law enforcement. I was radically mistaken.

Within twenty-four hours, the authorities contacted me, and mere days later I was speaking with a detective from the Crimes

---

* I've learned that doing internet searches to understand the law should be left to layers, the same way doing internet searches for illnesses should be left to doctors. Google is a terrible replacement for law school and medical school.

Against Children unit of the Arlington, Texas, police department. We met several times over the course of the next couple of months, and less than four months after my initial report, Mark was arrested and charged with three felonies: one count of sexual assault with a child under the age of seventeen and two counts of indecency with a child—sexual contact.

On December 19, 2018, he was indicted on those three felonies along with another count of indecency with a child—sexual contact. On July 2, 2019, he was charged with a fifth crime, assault causing bodily injury, a class A misdemeanor, to which he pleaded guilty.* With my husband by my side, my family and about a dozen friends in the gallery, I read him a victim impact statement telling him how the abuse affected me emotionally and spiritually. Even though I told him I wanted to look him in the eyes and let him know I forgave him, his eyes never left the floor. You can read the victim statement in its entirety at annemariemiller.com/statement. Before coming forward, I had no idea how complicated the criminal justice system is. After walking through the last year and a half with the detectives and attorney's office, I trust the process in which this decision was reached.

In July 2018 I chose to go public with my story. Because Mark had served overseas in Eastern Europe and had taken several trips—at least one solo—to Southeast Asia, I knew he had access to vulnerable people. I was even told he worked directly with victims of sex trafficking. I want to believe I was his only victim, and maybe I am. But the Christian organization had

---

* He received maximum sentencing for this crime, including jail time. However, if he follows the terms of his probation, his record will be expunged. While the internet is full of news about his criminal charges, any background checks will turn up clean. This is one reason why we can't rely on only background checks when we hire people or enlist volunteers.

never investigated his ministry, and in fact, I learned he was never terminated at all—he resigned. The organization knowingly allowed me to believe he was fired. While they were technically right to inform me that he was "no longer employed" with them, in context it came off as if they were acting to right something wrong. In reality, they simply let him resign and move on, refusing to acknowledge the criminal nature of his abuse—even saying in press releases that they wouldn't disclose the investigation for fear that they might get sued.

When my story and Mark's arrest went public and was reported in the media, thousands of people demanded a response from the SBC and this specific organization. Both entities remained largely silent. The organization issued a few generic statements, but the online community of abuse supporters demanded that more action be taken.

At the end of July 2018, the interim president of the organization when the story about Mark first broke was overseas. On his return, he and Dr. Russell Moore, the president of the SBC's Ethics and Religious Liberty Commission, personally called me to apologize and talk about what had happened and what I now needed. The organization's president, David Platt, issued a statement saying they would open every sexual misconduct case and have an objective third party make sure crimes were reported. He promised me they would investigate Mark's tenure overseas to see whether there were any other victims. Because sexual abuse has been at the forefront of discussion within the church, J. D. Greear, the new president of the SBC, made a statement the following day saying he would launch an initiative to improve how the church responds to sexual misconduct and how the SBC can do a better job at responding to sexual abuse. The organization where Mark served is actively combing through Mark's history, looking for more potential victims, and reporting all prior abuse cases to authorities, as well as following all recommendations made to them by a third-party independent examination.

Today I am encouraged and hopeful that the church—or at the very least the SBC—is starting to head down the right track. We're still early in this unfolding story, but I am trusting that good things will come.

Chapter 2

The Different Types of Abuse

To get us started, let's begin with some important statistics, definitions, and helpful tools to better understand sexual abuse. According to the National Center for Victims of Crime:

- Nearly 70 percent of all reported sexual assaults (including assaults on adults) occur against children ages seventeen and under.[1]
- One in five girls and one in twenty boys is a victim of child sexual abuse.
- Self-report studies show that 20 percent of adult females and 5 to 10 percent of adult males recall a childhood sexual assault or sexual abuse incident.
- During a one-year period in the US, 16 percent of youth ages fourteen to seventeen had been sexually victimized.

- Over the course of their lifetime, 28 percent of US youth ages fourteen to seventeen had been sexually victimized.
- Children are most vulnerable to childhood sexual abuse between the ages of seven and thirteen.[2]

Abuse Basics

When I share my story, I generally say I was "sexually abused," because that's a broad enough description to indicate that I was the victim of a crime without going into specifics. If the situation is appropriate, I will elaborate that the man who abused me was indicted for "indecency with a child" and "sexual assault." At this point in my life and healing, if someone were to ask me what those statements mean, I would generally be okay with elaborating. But that wasn't the case until recently. In appendix C, I've listed a lot of legal terms and definitions you can brief yourself on for the purpose of communicating with survivors and also to help you know when you should report something you've heard, seen, or know about. A fair warning: appendix C is not light reading.

I'll use some more general terms here regarding sexual abuse. It's important to know the differences in this language. Nuance can sometimes mean the difference between life or death and criminal or inappropriate. In many situations, especially in religious publications and statements, abuse is wrongly called "an inappropriate relationship." In my case, the language the Christian organization used—"Mark pursued an inappropriate sexual relationship with Miller"—was both morally and criminally inaccurate. This chapter is dedicated to helping you understand that phrases like these can be misleading, further protecting abusers instead of the public.

Mark did not "pursue a relationship" with me. He groomed me and abused me and committed a crime. And others are doing the very same thing to vulnerable people all over the world. Understanding the differences in these things will help you as you converse with sexual abuse survivors and discern whether to report a situation you know about.

Here are some helpful definitions from the National Center for Victims of Crime:

Accuser: Someone who imputes blame or guilt.

Affair: A sexual relationship between two adults. *Affair* is commonly used to denote a sexual relationship between two or more adults when at least one of them is in a committed relationship with another adult. This term also presumes that both adults consent.

Grooming: A process of identifying and engaging a person in unwanted or illegal abusive sexual activity. It involves an imbalance of power and elements of coercion and manipulation. It involves motivation and intent to sexually exploit the child. It is a process of desensitization.

Illicit sexual behavior: Takes place between a legal adult and usually a child of less than eighteen years of age in most states.[3] These sexual activities are intended to erotically arouse the legal adult, without consideration for the reactions or choices of the child. Behaviors that are sexually abusive often involve bodily contact such as sexual kissing, touching, fondling of genitals, and oral, anal, and vaginal intercourse. Behaviors may also be sexually abusive despite a lack of contact, such as genital exposure ("flashing"), verbal pressure for sex, and sexual exploitation for pornography or prostitution. This is a fairly broad term and varies from state to state.

Inappropriate activity: Behavior, often sexual in nature, that is not suitable considering the relationship status. Inappropriate activity might take place between a college professor and a student or a superior and his or her employee. It is generally used when referring to two consenting adults.

Inappropriate contact: Touching or contact that is not suitable for the time and place. Often used to describe either workplace touching or extramarital touching. This term should never be used to describe an adult touching a child.

Indecent liberties: Engaging in any of the following acts with a child who is fourteen or more years of age but less than sixteen years of age:

1. Any lewd fondling or touching of either the child or the offender, done or submitted to with the intent to arouse or to satisfy the sexual desires of either the child or the offender, or both; or
2. soliciting the child to engage in any lewd fondling or touching of another person with the intent to arouse or satisfy the sexual desires of the child, the offender, or another person.

Molestation: Commonly understood as the act of an adult subjecting a child in any type of sexual activity. Child molestation is a crime involving a range of indecent or sexual activities between an adult and a child.

Polyvictimization: Having experienced multiple victimizations of different kinds rather than just multiple episodes of the same kind of victimization. Also known as "multiple victimization" or "multivictimization."

Rape: The penetration, no matter how slight, of the vagina or anus with any body part or object, or oral penetration by a sex organ of another person or an item used for the perpetrator's sexual gratification (such as a sex toy, but can be any object), without the consent of the victim.

Revictimization: When a victim of a crime is subjected to either the same or a different type of crime or traumatizing experience. Many victims suffer revictimization by a different perpetrator within a short time frame. For instance, a person is victimized by one person and another person performs the same or different sexual act or abuse shortly thereafter. Revictimization can also include the process of re-living or re-experiencing the trauma mentally and emotionally. Asking the victim questions about his or her assault in

Asking the victim questions about his or her assault in a way that is not trauma-informed can cause revictimization.

a way that is not trauma-informed can cause revictimization. When the revictimization does not include a physically or sexually abusive act, it is generally not a crime.

Sexual abuse: A general term used to describe the infliction of some sort of sexual activity on a person who has not given consent or is incapable of giving such consent, such as people who are differently-abled, a child, or an elderly person.

Sexual relationship: A relationship involving sexual intimacy between two or more consenting adults. Can never be used to refer to a child since a child does not have the capacity to make a consenting choice to engage in sexual activity.[4]

It helps to be familiar with each term and to understand what it does and does not mean. As you can see, sexual abuse is a broad and general term that characterizes unwanted sexual activity of any kind. Other terms, such as rape or molestation, refer to more specific types of sexual abuse.

Types of Abuse

While this book focuses on sexual abuse, it's important to understand that there are several different kinds of abuse, and to note that they often overlap. Sexual abuse can also be physically abusive and violent. Spiritual abuse or spousal abuse can also be pieces of a sexually abusive relationship. Before we look at the various types of abuse, let's start with a few principles that every Christian should agree on:

All abuse is wrong.

All abuse is unbiblical.

All abuse is evil.

Most abuse is criminal.

SPIRITUAL ABUSE

Many books have been written about spiritual abuse. Spiritual abuse can come in many forms. It can be something as seemingly innocent as a sermon that is intentionally misleading or as drastic as a cult leader manipulating his followers. Regardless, it always belittles and demeans a person's value and worth using one of the most intimate parts of that person—their belief system.

Spiritual abuse is especially tricky because many people mistakenly identify a priest, pastor, or ministry leader as being "God's man" or "God's woman"—those who somehow hear directly from God in ways that regular people can't. Of course, this isn't true, given that God provides anyone access to him through Christ. But in cases when someone is new to the faith or lacks spiritual discernment and an abusive personality sees a vulnerability, abusers use their power to exploit it for their gain: whether that be financial, sexual, or emotional.

Spiritual abuse skews a person's perspective on reality, especially their perception of their relationship with God. Those who have been sexually abused by a pastor often don't trust the church, or ministry leaders, ever again. I've experienced firsthand the effects of spiritual abuse, and I can confirm that trust is really difficult. Almost every time I pass a church while I'm driving, I start imagining all the horrible things that might be going on there, even if the church is otherwise healthy. I don't *want* to view the church this way, but because my abuse had a spiritual component to it, my brain switches to survival mode, and I imagine reruns of what happened to me, making it difficult to look at anything of a religious nature without a negative response. It's impossible for many people who have been spiritually abused to see their faith and belief in God without being influenced by their abuse.

Another factor in spiritual abuse is the way in which well-meaning churches try to engage the abuse. Christians and churches may come alongside sexual abuse survivors with the best intentions, but those with good intentions may have a poor understanding of how trauma has rewired the abuse survivor. Their words or actions may cause even more damage to the body, mind, and spirit of the sexual abuse survivor. In saying this, I'm not assigning blame to people or churches trying to help in good faith. It's simply an unfortunate consequence that stems from the brokenness of abuse, a delicate and tender nuance to the process of recovery.

Spiritual abuse skews a person's perception of their relationship with God.

So how can you help an abuse survivor who has been spiritually abused? Instead of offering verses plucked from the Bible or an obligatory prayer, simply offer them your presence. Spend time sitting with them, listening, and asking what is needed. For most of us who have survived abuse, we need a safe place. It may be a place to simply stay for the weekend and decompress. We may want to watch a movie and get our minds off the memories and the pain for a while. We may want to go grab some food or coffee. We may want to sit in silence with you as we scroll on our phones for distraction (let's be honest). There is no magic cure for recovery from abuse—it's going to take a lot of time, and a lot of different things will be needed at various moments. Simply sit and ask us what we need in this moment, and more than likely, we'll answer you if we can and will thank you for asking.

PHYSICAL ABUSE

Physical abuse is what most people think of when they hear the word *abuse*. Physical abuse is any physical contact that is unwanted, intrusive, violent, and/or causes pain, injury, or other damage. Dr. William C. Shiel Jr. agrees, defining physical abuse as "the result of punching, beating, kicking, biting, burning, shaking, or otherwise harming."[5]

Physical abuse is caused by bodily contact or by an object. It can happen in all sorts of ways—someone throwing something at another person, kicking, punching, slapping, twisting, pushing, grabbing, choking, holding down, and so on. Some put spanking one's children in this category, though this topic is debated in many situations and circumstances. The detriment of physical abuse goes beyond the body and can affect other aspects of a person's being. Physical abuse can happen *to* anyone of any age or sex, *by* anyone of any age or sex.

EMOTIONAL ABUSE

Emotional abuse is very complex. It can be overt, such as withholding love and affection, and it includes bullying, name-calling, or degrading another person in any way. Emotional abuse is commonly a direct result of other abuses a person suffers. For example, physical abuse can cause emotional damage, as does any other kind of abuse. It can also work the other way around—the abuse may begin as emotional, then escalate over time and lead to physical abuse. The National Domestic Violence Hotline describes emotional abuse as "calling you names, insulting you or continually criticizing you, trying to isolate you from family or friends, demanding to know where you are every minute, punishing you by withholding affection, threatening to hurt you, the children, your family or your pets, damaging your property when they're angry (throwing objects, punching walls, kicking doors, etc.), humiliating you in any way, attempting to control your appearance: what you wear, how much/little makeup you wear, etc., telling you that you will never find anyone better, or that you are lucky to be with a person like them."[6]

Emotional abuse can also be subtle. People can be manipulative, controlling, or condescending. There are those who spin what happens in a situation in a confusing way. A common term associated with emotional abuse is something called *gaslighting*. When someone "gaslights" another, they use words to manipulate them, causing the victim to question their own sanity and reality. This may sound like a difficult thing to do, but it's actually simple. When you have a pathological narcissist—someone with an inflated and ego-centric sense of their own abilities—doing the talking, they will naturally turn the conversation to elevate and justify themselves and lay blame on others. Someone in my family was a victim of gaslighting by a pastor who made him question everything. He even experienced a slight bout of paranoia. He and his wife are both intelligent, educated, and extremely healthy people, but the pastor had them questioning whether their phones had been bugged and whether their house was under surveillance. It sounds unbelievable, but that is the power gaslighting has.

Emotional abuse is about controlling another person, sometimes in subtle and elusive ways. Emotional abusers are mental game-players, and their goal is to secure power over others.

SEXUAL ABUSE

We looked at a brief definition of sexual abuse earlier, so let's expand on that definition. Sexual abuse is any form of abuse where a person is used for another's sexual gratification. It is usually forced, though not always *physically* forced. Sometimes the abuse is emotionally forced, using fear, a position of power or authority, threats, grooming, manipulation, deceit, shame, or guilt. I know of a young woman who picked up some extra work as a dog walker so that she could save money to buy her kids a special Christmas gift. A man she worked for threatened to tell her husband they were having an affair if she didn't sleep with him. She resisted him at first, but he continued to threaten her and made her afraid that her husband wouldn't believe her. Sadly, she eventually broke down, and he used her fear to force her to have sex—even though she was physically compliant. In other cases, such as my own abuse as a teenager, an abuser can deceitfully manipulate another person to engage in sexual acts, exploiting their lack of discernment or age.

Remember, sexual abuse is always criminal, but many states have antiquated laws regarding consent and the statute of limitations, or how long a person has to report the abuse. Thankfully, many advocates are working tirelessly on improving laws to serve victims better.

FINANCIAL ABUSE

Financial abuse can sometimes fall within a spiritual or familial context. Is the church a good steward of the money that is given? Are necessary staff paid appropriately? Does a pastor or leader use guilt or promises of blessing outside Scripture to coerce congregants into giving? In a church my husband and I once attended, a pastor said on Good Friday, "If God sacrificed his Son for us, the least we could do is financially sacrifice for him!" While that's true—Jesus was a sacrifice for us—we knew this same pastor and his wife made hundreds of thousands of dollars in salaries in a relatively small church in a blue-collar town. We soon stopped attending that church.

Within a marriage, one spouse might control all the money and treat the other spouse like a child, demanding that all purchases be preapproved, maliciously causing the other spouse to feel guilty for spending money, or not allowing joint accounts for joint expenses. One spouse may take all the family's money and spend it unwisely without concern for the family or secretly hide it away for their personal use. There are endless examples, but one thing is true in each of them: using the power that comes from controlling the money to manipulate and harm another person.

DIGITAL ABUSE/HARASSMENT

Digital abuse is a relatively new form of abuse. Now that social media is accessible, widely used, and offers a measure of anonymity (and increased capability for unapologetic brashness without facing consequences), your everyday neighbor can spew vitriolic language online with almost no repercussions. Stating one's political opinion in hateful ways, bullying, lying, circulating nude photos without permission, threatening, and shaming others are now all too common. For some people, the insults and harassment roll off of them, and there's no problem hitting "block" and moving on. But having the ability to block another person does not mean you are no longer affected by hateful words. Hateful words deeply affect people—especially children and teens—and many take suggestions such as "you should just go kill yourself" literally. While there is a need to respect freedom of speech, this right must be balanced against the real harm words can cause, especially when used to incite hatred in others. There's no denying that our outrage culture is producing horrible, abusive fruit. As social media has risen in popularity, the number of suicides committed by kids under the age of eighteen has also increased. We must all be alert and aware of these trends and also eager to offer kind and supportive words online.

NEGLECT

Neglect brings to mind news stories of children found by Child Protective Services who have been locked away in closets or basements and starved of food, health care, and love. But while these are certainly cases of neglect, neglect can take on many other shapes and forms. Some may experience emotional neglect if they are not getting appropriate touch from parents or caregivers or not being affirmed by their family, and this can cause children long-term harm. I know a man who waited over twenty years before he heard his own mother say I love you to him, and this lack of verbal affirmation has scarred him and his relationships with others deeply. Even church leaders can be guilty of neglecting their congregations by not offering them guidance in their growth, by mishandling God's Word, or by withholding opportunities for relational connection. Spouses can withhold love and sex for control and power. These are all forms of neglect.

STALKING

Stalking is another form of abuse. It happens when someone repeatedly tries to contact you, follow you, threaten you, or initiate unwanted communication with you. It can happen physically, or it can take place online, as a form of digital abuse. There have been cases where pastors have stalked congregants for sexual or financial gain. Even married spouses can stalk each other with irrational jealousy. And there are many instances of adults stalking children and teens. As with other forms of abuse, we once again see the themes of power and control in each of these cases. The unwanted behavior, typically initiated by someone in a position of power over the victim, leaves the victim feeling powerless and ashamed.

Chapter 3

Who Are the Perpetrators?

The term we use to refer to the person committing the abuse is *perpetrator*. Sometimes people refer to perpetrators as *predators*, and while the word predator implies someone looking for prey—being strategic about who and when they will offend—it can also imply that the offender is unknown to the victim. Although many perpetrators are strategic and predatory, as we will learn below, a very small percentage of victims do not know the person who abuses them. So, for the sake of clarity and accuracy, we will use the word *perpetrator* to describe someone who sexually abuses another.

Who are perpetrators? What red flags do we look for? Can we always tell if someone is a perpetrator? How many victims do they have? Below are some basic facts regarding perpetrators offend:

- A small percentage of new child sexual abusers have a prior sex offense record, so it's incredibly difficult to track them.[1]
- Only 7 percent of child survivors were violated by an unknown perpetrator. [In other words, 93 percent of child abuse survivors knew their perpetrator.][2]
- Sixty percent of children are sexually abused by a family member or someone with whom they closely interact.
- Fourteen percent of sexual offenders commit another sexual offense within five years, and an additional ten percent reoffend between five and fifteen years.[3]

When you hear the word *pedophile* or *child abuser*, what's the image that comes to mind? Is it a mug shot of a gruff-looking man with sad or evil eyes, a five-o'clock shadow, and looks slightly creepy? Or maybe he just looks a little "off" somehow? These are common assumptions, but to better understand the types of people who can be predators, let's try the following exercise.

As you read the following phrases, picture the people who come to your mind as you read:

"He's such a good family man. There's no way he could have done this!"

"He would be the first person to report someone to authorities if he found out someone was sexually abused. He's the one who made me get a background check!"

"She's led the children's group for twenty years. There has never been a problem with her before. Those kids have to be making it up. She didn't touch them like that!"

"Have you heard him preach? A man of God like that would never go against Scripture."

The sad truth is that the people coming to mind right now are the typical profiles of those who sexually abuse children. Abuse is often committed by someone in a trusted position, an authority figure, someone who is respected by others, or a person in a position of power.

We teach our kids about "stranger danger," and while it is wise to do so, the statistics tell us that only 7 percent of sexually abused children don't know the person who abused them. This means that most of the abuse is not being committed by a creepy stranger but by a person the victim knows. Instead of being wary only of strangers, we need to teach our children to be aware of *everyone* around them. When we talk about childhood sexual abuse, or any form of abuse for that matter, we need to understand the *who*—the characteristics of a person who abuses someone—just as much as we need to understand *how*—the process predators use to find, groom, abuse, and silence their victims.

Abuse is often committed by someone in a trusted position.

The Who

Whether they are familiar to the victim or a stranger, perpetrators typically fall into one of these three categories:

1. *The strategic perpetrator.* This is the person who knows

exactly what he or she wants. They plan for their abuse and do everything they can to protect their image. These predators are those whom people find it difficult to believe that they would or could do anything wrong. That's because the perpetrator has carefully cultivated how they project themselves to the world. They are typically described as good guys, family guys, men of God, or other similar phrases, having developed a reputation for serving others. It might even be through serving the vulnerable. This develops trust and makes them less likely to be considered a perpetrator. The strategic perpetrator operates in plain sight because they don't feel any need to hide.

2. *The accidental perpetrator.* The accidental perpetrator is fairly uncommon, but he doesn't get a free pass. Unlike the strategic perpetrator, this individual doesn't plan a sex offense or look for opportunities to abuse someone. This person is likely immature in his faith and wisdom and makes several poor decisions over time. He may be a youth volunteer who doesn't think there's anything wrong with being alone in the youth room with a student in his Sunday school class as she confides in him. He may not even view her in a sexual manner. But maybe he struggles with looking at pornography, and over time he feels validated and fulfilled by the trust this girl is placing in him and becomes emotionally attached to her. Instead of pulling the plug and stopping the situation from developing in unhealthy ways, he ignores the warning signs and thinks he has it under control. The relationship progresses, and he initiates a physical and sexual relationship with her. Here is where we must have clarity. Just because he wasn't strategic in his abuse, it doesn't make him innocent of the crime he has committed. At some point, he crossed a line and chose to pursue an illicit relationship.

What he has done still needs to be brought to light and dealt with appropriately.

3. *The pedophile.* The pedophile is distinct from the strategic and accidental perpetrators. A pedophile is a person who has an active sexual preference and desire for children. Some pedophiles recognize that they are sick, and they place barriers and account-ability in their lives so they won't offend. Other pedophiles allow themselves some freedom to entertain and even cultivate these desires, and at some point they may "accidentally" offend. But some pedophiles strategically offend. The American Psychiatric Association defines *pedophilia* as a mental disorder, as "adults who are attracted to prepubescent children and may or may not be attracted to adults as well."[4]

Please understand that not all perpetrators are pedophiles and not all pedophiles are perpetrators. In addition, it's important to be aware that when we use words such as *pedophile* and *perpetrator,* we are naturally implying a degree of separation between that person and other people we know and are comfortable with. It's tough to identify someone we know as a *perpetrator or predator* because the word suggests that they are unable to control an animal instinct. Or it draws a mental picture of someone seeking their prey. But these pictures may not be accurate.

Why? Because perpetrators are dads, moms, brothers, sisters, uncles, aunts, coaches, teachers, pastors, janitors, doctors, nurses, neighbors, babysitters, daycare workers, friends, family, police, employees, employers, grocery store cashiers, waiters, baristas, students, lifeguards, camp leaders, youth leaders, and volunteers.

Anyone can be a perpetrator.

I don't write this to scare you unnecessarily, but I want to make you aware of your assumptions and prejudices. Because trauma colors the lens through which I see the world, when I scan a café, it's hard not to wonder whether anyone (everyone?) in there is a child molester. Statistically, it's all too likely that in a crowded café I am sharing the same air with an abuser, as well as several victims of abuse. And while we should not live in paralyzing fear, we must be on guard.

We must not let our fear of abuse bring harm to those we love.

The responsibility for vetting those in your church and those who have access to your family falls on you. And while it's scary to think of the different ways abuse might happen, it is possible to prepare in advance, taking simple steps that won't ruin your life. Sure, you could install cameras all over your house and never let your child out of sight, but if you lead your children like the world can't be trusted (regardless of how much you or I think that's true), it's guaranteed they will grow up with fear clouding their every interaction. That's not good. We can be cautious, but we must not let our fear of abuse bring harm to those we love. Fear can harm a child's intuition and ability to form relationships in the future.

My advice to you is to simply keep your eyes open.

Watch for red flags.

Act on those red flags.

When you act in good faith, you're not doing anything wrong.

The How

Experts have outlined what is widely referred to as "the grooming process," or a process by which strategic predators operate.

In almost all cases of strategic sexual abuse perpetrators follow this *modus operandi*: find the victim, earn their trust (and the trust of the family), exploit their vulnerability, and use them until you want to move on (or when you get bored or are almost caught).

In one large-scale study regarding child sexual abuse, researchers found offenders who took pride in their ability to find children to abuse. In almost every case, the offender targeted a child with unmet needs, often a need to be loved. Here are some of their comments:

> "I would probably pick the one who appeared more needy, the child hanging back from the others or being picked on by brothers and sisters."

> "I would find a child who didn't have a happy home life, because it would be easier for me to gain their friendship."

> "Choose children who will be unloved. Be nice to them until they trust you and then use love as a bait."

> "If you pick a kid who has been abused before, they'll think because you love them 'that this time it won't be as bad.'"[5]

> "In the process of grooming the child, you win his trust, and I mean, the child has a look in his eyes—it's hard to explain—you just have to kind of know the look. You *know* when you have that kid. You know when that kid trusts you."[6]

Is the Church More Vulnerable?

Perpetrators see churches as safe havens because the people in churches are often more willing to trust and believe the best of others. Churches are typically ill-equipped and poorly trained in this area, unable to see the warning signs of a potential perpetrator. And churches are, by definition, a sanctuary for the sick, hurting, and broken.

Dr. Anna C. Salter, PhD, is a psychologist who researches sex offenders. Her book *Predators: Pedophiles, Rapists, and Other Sex Offenders* is full of stories that take you a little too far into the minds of offenders. In her book she shares an uncomfortable and sickening truth, one that anyone seeking to prevent sexual abuse must hear. A predator who was also a minister confessed to her: "I considered church people easy to fool . . . they have a trust that comes from being Christians. . . . I think they want to believe in people. And because of that, you can easily convince, with or without convincing words."

Salter's research shows that most families are excited and honored when a priest or church leader takes an interest in their child. After all, who better to have as a role model than this man of God? In the mind of many parents is a belief that a pastor or church leader is an innocent, godly person. They are flattered at his interest in helping their family. It doesn't matter whether a church is structured in a patriarchal hierarchy or in more egalitarian ways; predators are able to easily move from church to church using different strategies.

Over and over again, Dr. Salter repeats what she has heard from predators—that church people are among the easiest to fool. One minister she interviewed was convicted of felony sex crimes and then released. He shared with her that he easily moved into another job at another church, working with children. *Working with children in another church.* But how does this happen?

First, he goes to the pastor.

"Do you take ex-cons?" he said meekly to a minister a few days after being released.

"Well, son, if they're truly repentant, we do."

"Oh, I am. . . . I was in Stevens Point for passing a cold check. You can check up on me if you don't believe me. And while I was there, I found the Lord, and there was this hymn I dearly loved. And I knew it would be a sign from God, whatever church was playing that hymn, that it was the church for me. . . . When I walked by your church this morning, you were playing that hymn."[7]

The pastor in this situation didn't check up on any of this story, of course. After all, if this person were a real criminal, he wouldn't have confessed his sin, disclosed his punishment, and suggested that the church could check up on his story, right? When law enforcement finally caught up to this man, he was serving in two churches. The pastor of the other church told authorities, "Well, we thought he was sincere. You see there was this hymn that he dearly loved in prison, and when he walked by our church . . ."[8]

Below is the transcript of an interview Dr. Anna Salter conducted with a convicted predator who was previously also a church leader.

PREDATOR: In the meantime, you're grooming the family. You portray yourself as a church leader . . . whatever it takes to make that family think you're okay. You show the parents you're really interested in that kid. You just trick the family into believing you are the most trustworthy person in the world. Every one of my victims, their families just totally thought that there was nobody better to their kids than me, and they trusted me wholeheartedly with their children.

SALTER: At church, you did not molest all the children at church. How did you choose?

PREDATOR: Ok . . . that's a good question. First of all you start the grooming process from day one . . . the children that you're interested in . . . You find a child that you might be attracted to . . . For me, it might be nobody fat. It had to be, you know, a nice-looking child, wasn't fat. I had a preference for maybe blonde hair but that didn't really have a lot to do with it.

You maybe look at a kid that doesn't have a father image at home. You know, you start deducing. Well, this kid may not have a father, or a father that cares about him. Some kids have fathers but they're not there with them . . .

Say if you've got a group of twenty-five kids, you might find nine that are appealing. Well, you're not going to get all nine of them. But just by looking, you've decided, just from the looks, what nine you want. Then you start looking at their family backgrounds. You find out all you can about them. Then you find out which ones are the most accessible. Then you eventually get it down to the one you think is the easiest target, and that's the one you do.

SALTER: How do you keep your victims from telling?

PREDATOR: Well, first of all I've won all their trust. They think I'm the greatest thing that ever lived. Their families think I'm the greatest thing that ever lived. Because

I'm so nice to them and I'm so kind and so—there's just nobody better to that person than me. If it came down to, you know, if it came down to, "I have a little secret, this is our little secret" then it would come to that, but it didn't usually have to come down to that. It's almost an unspoken understanding.

SALTER: Do you think any of the families ever became suspicious of you?

PREDATOR: I'm sure they become suspicious, but that's when I begin my grooming on the family again . . . If a family becomes suspicious, they're not really going to bring it to me.

They're going to bring it to their kid first. And the kid, I've got the kid so well groomed that the kid's going to bring it to me and say, "Well my mom asked me, you know, if you ever tried to do anything to me or anything like that."

Well, then I begin working on the family by still being kind of nice to them but maybe backing off of that child just enough to where that parents' suspicion gets back down. Maybe I'm not with them as much. I won't maybe have as much physical contact. I won't put my arm around the child as much. I'll do everything. Whatever it takes to convince the family that there's not a problem.

Salter tells us that this man admitted sexually abusing over one hundred victims. But what is most striking in this case is that only one victim told what had happened to him. After that child spoke out, other children's parents were in denial, not willing to let social services come near their child, not even to learn whether the child had been abused. They preferred to remain willfully ignorant. Surely *they* had not trusted their child with a sexual perpetrator. She writes: "Some families still write to him [the predator] in prison. He could *not* have been a child molester, and he most certainly never molested *their* child. After all, nobody was ever better to their child than he was."[9]

Her interview with this man ends with a haunting statement, one that should stay glued to our minds. He says to her, almost bragging: "Child molesters are very professional at what they do, and they do a good job at it."[10] *They are professional at what they do.* Sadly, we cannot overlook the reality that our churches are prime targets for people who are intent on targeting our children and loved ones to satisfy their illicit and illegal desires.

And in case you think these stories are unique, let's walk through some of the details of my own story once again.

- In my email to Mark, I said I was new to town and trying to start a See You at the Pole event at my school to meet some Christians. We didn't have a church or a youth pastor.
- He met my mom and me. They chatted about the seminary and missions—all common things. My mom knew he was helping me.
- He called to check on how See You at the Pole went, which was horrible because nobody showed up. I was going to give up on God, I thought.
- He asked whether I could come over to watch a movie and talk about it. This was a moment when he would learn whether he could get easy access to me. He could. I had access to a car, and my parents trusted me.
- He slowly progressed in physical touch with me, getting to know me, and I felt heard by him.

- As the abuse progressed sexually, he specifically asked whether I was a virgin and shared how he had lost his own virginity. Perhaps he was testing me, seeing how far I was comfortable going and if I was sexually active in my past.*
- At some point, he began to distance himself from me. Maybe his (to-be) wife was coming home for the holidays. Maybe he just had to go home. But something happened, and he pulled away. But when we talked, he made sure I knew he'd be back.
- After he returned and the abuse continued, he abruptly ended it. His (to-be) wife was coming back. She couldn't ever know what had happened.
- I turned him in to the Christian organization. He admitted spending time with me to some (to me, unknown still) extent, but not the whole thing. By admitting this, he was seeking to be truthful, disclosing something he could have kept secret, but it wasn't the full truth.
- After he was "caught" several years later with the organization's investigation, he managed to resign before he could be fired and brazenly applied to pastor a church in Arkansas. He listed professional and personal references from this organization. Why would he list them if he had something to hide?
- The organization was only allowed to share his salary and dates of employment. He did not sign a disclosure allowing them to share anything else. The new church didn't check his personal references (so I'm told). He was hired.

---

* Because he's never confessed to grooming me, I can't say for certain he was a strategic perpetrator. But the timeline and actions line up with the definition of grooming.

- He began working in a church two months after resigning from the organization for being credibly accused and determined to have sexually abused me. Over the next decade, he climbed the SBC ladder, winning people over with his giftedness and ability.
- When he was arrested, people couldn't believe it. When he was indicted, people still couldn't believe it. Even after he pleaded guilty to the misdemeanor, someone contacted me to remind me that he didn't plead guilty to the felony sex crimes, so he is innocent of those. Others have told me that the Christian organization and criminal investigations don't have all the information (they do).

Do you see a pattern emerging? The perpetrator identifies his potential victim, a vulnerable person. He builds rapport with family or friends and then begins spending time alone with the victim, developing trust. When confronted with his crime, he denies any wrongdoing, continuing to rely on the trust he has developed and the image he has cultivated.

Here, in the end, is why the church is more vulnerable than others to attacks by perpetrators. In churches, people want to believe the best about other people because, as Dr. Anna Salter reminds us in her book, the alternative to believing the best about people is not very nice.

Indeed, it isn't.

But unfortunately, as many churches have been learning recently, the alternative is all too true. And it comes at a high cost.

Church and State:
Is there a difference between criminal activity and immoral behavior?

I receive all sorts of emails—many of which condemn me for speaking about my abuse. Some try to tell me that I wasn't sexually abused because I was teenager—so I was "old enough to know better"—and the relationship wasn't physically forced. They argue that even if I was groomed or manipulated, at some level I *liked* Mark's attention at the time, so it's wrong for me to be complaining now. Others try to compare their own experiences to mine. Often they are comparing it to a sexual experience between two consenting adults, not an illicit relationship between a pastor and a teenage student.

All of this indicates to me a profound lack of knowledge about abuse, and it begs several questions: When is abuse considered a crime? When is a sexual relationship morally wrong? And when does a moral wrong become criminal activity?

For those interested, I've provided a list of terms commonly used in the US legal system in appendix C. Keep in mind that the laws vary from state to state, and what's considered a felony in one place may not be one in another. And the statute of limitations varies, so if survivors come forward after the time the law allows, an offender may not be charged with a crime. In some states, such as Texas, if a person in a position of authority, such as a pastor, counselor, doctor, teacher, caretaker, social worker, or law enforcement officer (to name a few), has unwanted sexual contact with anyone

When is abuse considered a crime?

of any age, it's a crime. But in some states, that isn't the case. For a list of what the laws say about sexual abuse in your state and how a crime is defined, the statute of limitations, and other important details about sex crimes and abuse laws, you can look up your state on the RAINN.org website or talk to your local law enforcement (RAINN is an abbreviation for Rape, Abuse & Incest National Network and is a partner with the US Department of Defense).

Recently, I was involved in a discussion with officials in a religious institution of higher education. They were discussing the idea of revoking degrees awarded to people who violated the institution's code of ethics while attending school. These individuals had deceived the school by covering up their sin, in some cases their crimes. Some thought the idea was too extreme and would open the institution up to a lawsuit. My thought was that if you are going to be sued, there is no better reason than for protecting the vulnerable and standing up for the justice of the abused. Others felt the revocation should happen only after the graduate had been convicted through the legal system. Again I weighed in, pointing out that not every act that violates a school's code of ethics is a crime, nor will all crimes get reported. Statistically, very few of these types of crimes are reported (230 out of 1,000), and even fewer lead to a felony conviction (4.6 out of 1000).[11] By imposing the requirement of a criminal conviction to determine whether an act constitutes abuse, we would be elevating a man-made system of justice over what we, as Christians, know and believe to be good and true.

Hear me clearly. We need to be aware of the laws in our own state. We need to know which acts constitute a crime and when we need to alert authorities. This is of vital importance, as it could mean the difference between life and death to someone in need. But we cannot stop there. We should not limit our actions to the minimum requirements of state or federal law and allow *only* the law of our land to define what is right or wrong, morally and ethically. We need the courage to look at each situation with the eyes of our conscience, led by the Holy Spirit, instructed in Scripture, and confirmed by others, all in addition to working with law enforcement when necessary.

Chapter 4

Survivors and Victims

*I*n a recent meeting, a pastor asked me a simple question: "What's the difference between a victim and a survivor?" His question reminded me that not everyone is well-versed in the terminology of abuse and recovery, and it also sent me on an interesting journey to learn more about the history of the words used to describe those who have suffered abuse and survived.

The easy answer to the pastor's question is that the two words are virtually synonymous. A victim is another way of referring to a survivor, and vice versa. Different terms are used depending on the context, and sometimes it is just a matter of preference and perspective. Here is a simple rule you can apply when you are supporting an abuse survivor: just ask him or her which term is preferred.

The word *victim* tries to accurately communicate the horror of sexual abuse. Originally from the Latin word *victima*, the term *victim* was used to describe someone who was killed in a religious sacrifice. In many instances, I think it is appropriate to refer to those who have suffered sexual abuse as victims because it highlights the pain and horror of that sacrifice. From the first moment sin entered the world in Eden, evil has demanded a sacrifice.* In the case of sexual abuse, the victim is sacrificed to the sexual desire of the perpetrator. It takes tremendous strength to survive abuse—the forceful, sometimes violent, unwanted theft of one's body, mind, and spirit.

Similarly, the word *survivor* also has an interesting history. It is derived from two Latin words: *vivere*, "to live," and the prefix *sur*, or *super*, meaning "over, beyond." A survivor is someone who lives over and beyond the trauma of their abuse. It communicates the hope of moving beyond the pain of the past and is an attempt to shape a new narrative and tell a new story.

A survivor is someone who lives over and beyond the trauma of their abuse.

Frequently, legal settings will use the word *victim* to denote a person who has suffered a wrong and needs justice. But many support groups and counselors will use the term *survivor* because it reshapes the narrative that we who have suffered abuse tell ourselves and the world. I find both terms helpful because, more often than not, we live each day with a dual tension. We deeply sense the sacrifice forced on us as victims and acknowledge the injustice we have experienced, while fighting with all we have to live as survivors. My friend Brad describes the paradox this way: "Both words are true in describing us, but not in defining us. We who have

---

* "The LORD God made garments of skin for Adam and his wife and clothed them" (Genesis 3:21). The depiction of an animal blood sacrifice is made here. Blood had to be shed in order to protect Adam and Eve from the world now that it was not the perfect, original creation.

endured abuse are victims of others' activities, yet survivors with our own identities. Despite someone else's *activity*, we don't have to integrate our *identity* around them. This helps us distinguish why survivors sometimes talk about victimization, and sometimes about survivorship and recovery, shifting terms as befits the context."*

Why Do Survivors Wait to Talk?

Why do abuse victims often wait to talk about their abuse? Why don't they report it right away? The reasons will vary from person to person, and it is up to a survivor to determine the when and the how of telling their story, if they choose. The role of a supporter is not to force someone to share but to create a safe place, free of judgment, so that survivors know there are people who care *if* they decide to share.

In my book *5 Things Every Parent Needs to Know about Their Kids and Sex*, I offered two reasons behind a survivor's decision not to come forward: fear and shame. And as I've studied abuse and trauma as a nursing student, I've learned about the physiology of our brains and how our memory plays a significant role in the decision to talk. As difficult as it is for some people to accept this, sometimes survivors don't talk when they are first abused because they don't remember. (See appendix B for more information on memory.)

REASON #1: FEAR

Many survivors are afraid to talk about what has happened to them. They may be afraid because they think no one will believe

---

* Brad Sargent is known as @futuristguy on Twitter. Brad researches, analyzes, and documents systemic abuse on his website at futuristguy.wordpress.com. Two thumbs up.

them, or they may feel as if they are somehow to blame. Sadly, this fear is often realized when they share publicly. When I began talking about my own story of abuse, a woman emailed me to say I should have "known better" and because I "allowed" the sexual activity to continue, what happened to me was not abuse (even though the law disagrees). This woman clearly did not understand that sexual abuse has mental, emotional, spiritual, and physical dimensions. Confusing and manipulating the victim emotionally is just as much a part of an abuser's strategy as physical touch. And we should not ignore the power dynamics at work in relationships between children and adults and those in positions of authority who use their position to exploit others.

Victims of sexual abuse may also be afraid of getting someone in trouble. This is very common with children. The victim may transfer the responsibility for the abuse from the abuser to themselves. When I found myself having to talk to investigators about my abuse, I kept thinking, "I don't want to break up his family or ruin his marriage. How will his wife feel? What will happen to his kids?" It was not easy for me to move beyond this fear, and it took years of therapy to accept and believe that I am not responsible for the repercussions that result from the abuse I experienced. It's the abuser who decides to take advantage of the victim, and the victim is not responsible for the impact that decision may have on the abuser or his future. Some days I wish this fear were something that could be easily left behind, but this just points to the deep psychological impact of sexual abuse and how damaging it can be to the victim.

Over the years, I've heard stories of sexual abuse that occurs within a family unit. Frankly, there's nothing more terrifying for a person—especially a child—than to face the possibility that he or she might break up the family or might be cast out from the family altogether. So there is a strong incentive to cover it up and refrain from speaking. Again, I would stress that pressure to speak out (beyond what is necessary for reporting the abuse to authorities) should not be placed on any victim, whether a child or an adult.

REASON #2: SHAME

Because of the discomfort many have in talking about sexual abuse, and our tendency to link sex with feelings of guilt or embarrassment, victims of sexual assault may have a significant amount of shame. Often people who have been sexually abused believe they are used, dirty, and worthless. They tend to see themselves as weak, vulnerable, naive, and even stupid. Even saying the word *abuse* was difficult for me at first, and it happened only after *a lot* of time and practice. Those who are victims are continually wondering: what man or woman would ever love someone who has been violated in such an intimate way? No one wants to be seen as weak or vulnerable, stupid or naive, yet that's how many people view themselves after they have been abused.

I felt shame when I thought of other people speculating about the details of my abuse, and I didn't want people to think I was stupid or naive. At times, I questioned my own intelligence. Prior to the abuse, I was an honors student who earned straight As and received scholarship offers. But I told myself that if I were really all that smart, I would never have let this happen to me. I questioned why I had failed to tell someone about the abuse. Even later, I wondered why it took me until my twenties to understand that what had happened was *abuse*. Today I know that my lack of knowledge about how abuse works, coupled with the shame of being a victim and the sexual nature of my abuse, kept me locked in a place of fear. the shame compelled me to keep the abuse I had experienced a secret from others.[1]

REASON #3: MEMORY

There are times, especially in abuse cases that involve children, when a process called disassociation occurs. Disassociation removes the mental consciousness from what the physical body is going through or experiencing. It is a primal form of survival. Children cannot consciously handle sexual abuse, so the body shuts down the ability to remember what is happening. Many years later, something—a sight, a smell, or an experience—may trigger the consciousness again and cause the brain to "unlock" the hidden memory. The person, usually an adult at this point, will begin to remember the event. The lesson we can draw from this is that even when we may not cognitively remember abuse, our bodies don't forget. As Dr. Bessel van der Kolk says, "Trauma literally reshapes both body and brain, compromising sufferers' capacities for pleasure, engagement, self-control, and trust."[2]

It's also not uncommon for victims to forget certain details while remembering others in recounting their sexual abuse experience. Many survivors have a strong sense when something has been forgotten and stored away. Our bodies remember even when our minds do not, and when it's "safe" for us to remember again, our bodies let us know. Because we can access some fragments of our memory but not all of them, this can be confusing and scary when it first happens. Remembering forgotten memories may cause a survivor to question their experience. The memories themselves *and* the realizing that we have forgotten something and later remembered it is itself terrifying. Many survivors wonder: *If I forgot this part, what else am I forgetting?* There may be nothing scarier than not being able to remember what you've been through, especially when it's something as painful and personal as sexual abuse. Sometimes when these memories come back again, they are full of detail.[3] I have personally experienced a surge of forgotten memories. When I was driving in Fort Worth, I passed the apartments Mark lived in. It had been years since I saw them. I instinctively knew where his apartment was and drove to it. A flood of memories hit me so hard my body went into shock, and I had to have my husband, who was an hour and a half away, come to drive me home.

Our bodies remember even when our minds do not.

As someone who may be caring for survivors, you need to understand that many survivors forget their abuse, including many details of it, and thus feel as if they can't come forward. However, *not* having certain memories because they are associated with trauma is extremely common. Help a survivor accept that this may have happened. Eventually, if the person feels safe enough, they may begin to remember again. Do everything you can to be a safe place for them. The safer they feel, the more likely they will be able to process the memories their bodies have stored because they've previously felt unsafe.

Understanding
the Basics of Trauma

There has been a great deal of controversy about survivors who talk of their abuse, sometimes years or even decades after the event. As I stated previously, fear and shame may keep someone from sharing. And in some cases, there can be repressed memories due to disassociation of the mind and body during the abuse. Yet most people still wonder: if this event was really so traumatic, wouldn't the individual *want* to tell someone, to report it to authorities and get help? The answer to that question is not always as straightforward and simple as it seems. Research on memory and the effects of traumatic events can help us better understand what is happening in the mind of a survivor and why they may be reluctant to talk. (For more information on trauma, see appendix B.)

While researching the effects of trauma on a survivor, I've uncovered several studies that can help us better understand how trauma plays a role in survivors' silence. We'll look at some of those studies, but we'll begin by unpacking the fundamental response to trauma. In living creatures, this response is known as *fight-flight-freeze-fawn*.[4] These actions are what we instinctively do when faced with a traumatic or painful experience. Sometimes, depending on our age or maturity, our mind may respond one way and our body may respond another. We never know when or how a traumatic event will happen, and the response to it is as equally unpredictable.

To unpack the four responses, let's imagine you're walking along on the sidewalk with a baby in a stroller. A bear (yes, a bear) runs at you. What do you do? The answer to that question will vary from person to person and situation to situation, and most of the time we don't have an ounce of control how we respond. Let's consider each of the four options.

Fight: In this scenario you jump between the bear and stroller and start lashing out with an unseen fury, kicking and yelling and hitting. You throw your diaper bag at it (that bag is heavy—those twenty-five pounds of stale Cheerios and Goldfish in it actually come in handy).* You growl. You scream. And you do this all without thinking.

Flight: With superhuman power you pick up the stroller and run as fast as you can to the safest spot you can find.

Freeze: You stop. You stop talking. You stop moving. You completely freeze. If the bear thinks you're a statue, maybe he'll just keep moving. Your body freezes too, conserving energy, heat, and slowing your metabolism . . . it's as close to being not alive as you can be in a conscious state. Some might say it's your body's way of "playing possum" in an effort to save your life.

Fawn: Fawning is a newer addition to the list of initial trauma responses. To *fawn* means to appease your attacker. You become compliant in an attempt to get the attack to stop. With the bear, perhaps you pull out the Goldfish crackers from the diaper bag and toss them over to the bear as a peace offering. Your voice pitches up to singsong, and you tell the bear how nice he is. You squat down on the ground to show you're not a threat. You do whatever it takes to convince the bear that he's the one in control and you're okay with him being there, even though you are most definitely *not* okay with that.

If you look throughout nature, you'll see that all animals respond to trauma in one of these ways. The difference between humans and other animals is the conscious level at which we process what happens to us and our resulting complex emotions. Have you ever seen a dog shake after getting riled up or during a thunderstorm? That's their body's way of releasing trauma: they experience it, process it neurologically, and once it doesn't serve them any longer, they let it go (often by shaking or another

---

* At least that's what's in my daughter's diaper bag.

physical expression). As they shake, neurons fire and the trauma essentially shoots out through their various systems and out of their skin (kind of like the way we get goosebumps when something eerie happens: same idea). Something similar happens when someone is sexually abused. Sometimes a victim exhibits one or more of these four responses. In my case, I found that my responses were *freeze* and *fawn*. I had so many fears and other emotions run through my body when Mark began escalating our physical contact that I froze. When I appeased him, in my situation a subconscious choice, I continued to let him take the intimate actions further.

> *The trauma that stays with us wreaks havoc until we process it and walk through a journey of healing.*

When trauma strikes, our response is determined by a variety of factors, many beyond our immediate control. Because of our individual genetics, experiences, and temperaments, some ordeals are ones we can "shake off," while others that are more severe stick with us longer. The trauma that stays with us after it has served its purpose tends to wreak havoc on our bodies and our minds over time until we process it and walk through a journey of healing. Since each one of us is unique, that journey of healing is shaped as uniquely as we are.

The good news is that healing is available. And once we understand the depth of our trauma, we can climb out of its reach, inch by inch. In the next section we'll look even further into how trauma works so you, as a supporter of someone who has been abused, are better equipped to meet and serve your loved one.

Chapter 5

Understanding the
Role of Supporters

While the overall goal of this book is to help people understand abuse, trauma, and how to help those who have experienced the horror of sexual abuse, we would be remiss to miss the *why* in all this: so that a world will know the love of Christ. As Galatians 6:2 says, "Carry one another's burdens; in this way you will fulfill the law of Christ" (CSB).* In verse 5 he says, "For each person will have to carry his own load" (CSB). In essence, because each one of us is charged to bear our own weight, when we do lift another's, we are doing the work of God—we are setting an example of love for the world to see. And in the process, we are directly affecting the healing of another, showing compassion, light, and love where the enemy has caused deep and tremendous pain.

---

* Paul is talking about helping restore other believers after they have chosen to misstep.

I was only five years old when my mom told me to jump into the deep end of Aunt Sharon and Uncle Jesse's pool for the first time (yes, I have an Uncle Jesse, and no, it's not John Stamos). She said she'd catch me. My mom grew up in Hawaii, spending her youth barefoot on a houseboat and wore water like a second skin. I was born and raised in Texas, landlocked and clumsy.

I was nervous and tense, and my tiny toes wrapped the curved cement edge. "Just go!" my cousin, also five years old but an expert diver, urged as she bounced at the end of the diving board, waiting for my mom—and me—to clear her way. I unfurled my toes and closed my eyes, and I jumped. As I closed my eyes and hit the water, my mom moved to the left, a premeditated attempt to get me to learn how to swim. I bobbed up, gasping for air and thrashing, only for a moment, before sinking again. My mom reached to grab me and pull me to safety, but my long limbs and adrenaline pushed her five-foot frame underwater. My dad and uncle came to help. It took three adults to bring a forty-pound kindergartner to safety.

That's what trauma does: it plunges one person underwater without warning, and as she fights to survive, those nearest to her try to bring her to safety—and it's not easy. Experts warn people who are drowning to be as still as possible—so lifeguards can save them. When a crisis hits us, more often than not, our emotions spin out of control, and we need help as we thrash in the water, dipping below the surface. Your presence can keep us afloat, breathing and surviving the experience.

People with good intentions can jump into the water and try to help, but everyone may end up drowning because they don't know the basics of helping someone who's drowning. Or sometimes moving beyond jumping into the water seems too daunting, so we stay on the side of the pool, horrified (but praying! Sooo many thoughts and prayers!). Some want to jump in but honestly don't know what to do, so they stay inside, looking through the patio doors, never making their presence known.

There's no one specific person who is the only person charged with saving us, but relationships are absolutely needed in order to heal. I believe there are three categories of relationships necessary to fully support the healing of a survivor: family and friends, a broader community such as a church or a support group, and professionals. Every relationship brings a unique element of healing and support, and every relationship helps keep survivors from drowning in trauma. Sometimes survivors may not want to engage with one or more

Every relationship helps keep survivors from drowning in trauma.

of these. Perhaps they aren't close to their family or are new and don't know many people. Maybe a church community is out of the question, or the idea of going to therapy is off-putting or (unfortunately) not affordable. Allow the survivor to express what relationships they feel they need, and help them find them.

In my book *Lean on Me*, I describe three types of relationships:

- Committed but not vulnerable: you're faithful to the people around you, no matter what, but you're not open about your struggles.
- Vulnerable but not committed: you're completely open about your struggles, but you're not committed to any one group of people for growth.

- Committed and vulnerable: this is the ideal relationship to have with someone. You're intentionally committed to each other, and you're vulnerable with each other. This is the sweet spot, where growth happens. And it's not only for our own sake, but it shows a hurting world that we—followers of Christ—actually mean business when we say we love people.[1]

The Role of Family and Friends

The role of family and friends is unique. Generally, family and friends (close friends, not acquaintances) already know the survivor and are typically in the "committed" category of relationships. There are people in my family I don't sign up to spend time with, but I know in those milestone events in life—births, deaths, illness, holidays—we're going to be around each other. The same is true for some of my friends.

Whether or not we are committed *and* vulnerable depends on the relationship with the person. Some families are closer than others, and different relationships have different dynamics. There are things I tell my husband that I'd never tell anyone else. There are things I tell my best friends that I don't tell anyone else. When it comes to my abuse, sometimes I feel more comfortable sharing with someone who has a similar experience.

The summer after my book tour, when I finished my season of intensive counseling, I had a group of friends, but most fell in either committed relationships or vulnerable relationships. There were few people in the sweet spot of committed and vulnerable. I was asking a friend for advice on how I could continue healing, and he suggested I intentionally ask a small group of people—for me, it was about twelve—if they would commit to walking alongside me for the next eighteen months, helping me stay accountable to my healing. I went through my address book, and once I picked the people, I wrote them individual emails asking directly for their support, baring the areas I especially needed help in. In a way, it was like writing a note to a grade school crush: do you like me? Circle one: yes or no.

Will you commit to being my friend—committed and vulnerable—for the next eighteen months?

Ten of the twelve people affirmed they would, and I learned that the intentionality behind my ask, as well as inviting them into specific areas of my life that needed growth, really helped me heal for the next year and a half. It's been almost a decade since then, and while I'm not in day-to-day relationships with most of them anymore, we share a special bond from walking with each other during that time.

More than likely, abuse survivors may find it difficult to reach out and ask for help in such a specific way. The topic is too tender. Especially directly after the abuse or after coming forward with it, survivors are emotionally exhausted, ashamed, and think they'll be a burden on someone. If you already know that your relationship with the survivor you're helping falls in the "committed and vulnerable" category, you're in an ideal spot: you're a trusted person and a safe place. If you're not sure or you're not close to them, it would be beneficial to ask whether they have people in their life that they're able to be vulnerable with and committed to. Ask who they feel comfortable enlisting to help and whether you're able to reach out to those people on their behalf. Let them know you're fully available to commit to walking alongside them.

The Church's Role

As I mentioned earlier, though my experience happened in a particular denomination, sexual abuse isn't a denominationally specific issue.

It's not even only a church problem.

It's a *human* problem. It's an *evil* problem.

As someone aptly said to me after sharing that sentiment on social media: before the church can help us heal, the church must do no harm. The church must be the force to bring light and healing to those harmed by sexual abuse. Someone once said, "Just because it's not your fault doesn't mean it's not your responsibility."

In cases where the church *is* at fault, it must be responsible for helping facilitate the healing of those harmed by sexual abuse. In cases where the church is *not* at fault, it is still responsible for helping facilitate the healing of those harmed by sexual abuse. But that assumes the survivor is looking to the church for help.

The role the church plays in a survivor's healing can vary widely. Some survivors run to the church because it is a safe place for them and they find encouragement in the life and community of a church. Others, like me, are more hesitant to darken the doors of a church. I'm trying to find hope in the church again. I'm trying to open up and be trusting, but it's hard. It's likely there are many survivors who will never enter a church again.

Regardless of how strongly you may feel that a survivor needs to be a part of a church community or how certain you are that the church is essential to their healing, *please do not push the issue*. Honestly, I wouldn't even bring it up. It's okay to ask how someone feels about including the church as a party to their healing, but be ready to respect their answer. If someone isn't willing or ready to embrace the role of the church in their healing and you try—even in the smallest ways—to convince them otherwise, you will lose credibility with them. When someone overtly or subtly infers the necessity of my return to the institution of the church, it makes me feel as though I'm something broken that needs fixing. *Project Anne Marie: get her to go to church so she can reconnect with Jesus and heal.* Sorry. That isn't how it works.

I also want to briefly address the process of reconciliation between churches and survivors when the church, a denomination, or another religious entity was party to sexual abuse. If you're a leader in any way, no matter how small a role you feel you play, your actions carry great weight with survivors because your affiliation, no matter how slight, can represent the organization as a whole.

It's likely there are many survivors who will never enter a church again.

There have been pastors, convention executives, church members, and trustees—people with positions and roles all over the spectrum of the Southern Baptist Convention's denomination—who have contacted me to encourage me. In almost every case, they have each done something tangible (that they considered to be "small" in the grand scheme of things but were quite significant in my healing). Both actions—their reaching out and their act of simply letting me know they're there, unconditionally—have been some of the most encouraging and hopeful encounters I've experienced since coming forward with my abuse publicly.

For example, pastors have asked me what they can do in their churches to create safe places and have offered to write their SBC representatives letters on my behalf, demanding accountability and change. Executives have sought input on what policies they can suggest that the denomination should adopt or have voted in opposition to the status quo. A woman who is a member of an SBC church redirected her offerings to a different denomination because she felt as if her money was going to support an organization that was actively causing pain. Trustees of various boards have introduced new procedures and bylaws that will influence the denomination in a positive way for the foreseeable future.

Once, as I met with two local pastors who wanted to know how they could help, they did (or didn't do) something that caught me off guard. They didn't pray before or after our meeting. What I like to call the obligatory "sandwich prayer"—praying on the front end and at the close of a meeting—is predictable. I can't recall one time in any of my interactions with pastors in four decades when this didn't happen. But these two men, knowing how sensitive I am to "churchy" things, didn't bring in *any* agenda to our meeting other than to listen. I don't think badly of people who pray when I meet with them, but by not praying, their intentionality spoke volumes to me.

Does your church have the resources to help subsidize the costs of counseling? Are there attorneys in your church who can help survivors pro bono? Are you partnered with ministries that can provide safe childcare or even a place for a survivor to stay? One of the informal polls I did online asked about the cost of healing from sexual abuse. The answers ranged from $5,000 to over $500,000.* My own expenses fall in the average of those numbers, and that's just the cost of getting mental health treatment. It doesn't include physical care for ailments possibly brought

---

* I conducted this informal online poll and received responses from my and others' followers on social media. Forty people participated in this survey.

on by trauma. I asked some survivors whether the cost of services had prevented them from getting the mental health care they needed, and a majority of those surveyed responded yes.

I also asked both survivors and supporters how the church could best help with the cost of mental health services. A majority of supporters and survivors think the church should partner with licensed mental health professionals to offer free or discounted services, or even completely subsidize the cost for survivors.

Even if survivors aren't actively involved with you or your congregation, you can reach beyond the walls of your church and find ways to make a difference. These acts really do help survivors see beyond the pain and politics the church has caused, intentionally or not, over time.

Enlisting Professional Help

Mental illnesses, including those caused by trauma, should be considered a health problem like any physical illness. They require professional help and professional treatment in order to improve someone's quality of life, better their long-term outcomes, and offer continuing guidance on their healing journey.

In most cases of sexual abuse, the aid from licensed counselors and medical professionals is invaluable. In the Christian community, there are counselors and practitioners who have obtained professional degrees or certifications, indicating that an individual has gone through specific training. Some survivors may not be open to using a biblical counselor (personally, it's not for me) because they have lost any trust in institutional faith-based organizations. Instead of suggesting a biblical or Christian counselor, ask survivors whether they feel the need to get counseling or medical help, and if they do, ask them what kind of help they feel comfortable pursuing.

Remember, most victims have lost their voice—their say in what happens to them—and asking them this simple question helps affirm their own sense of self and agency, giving them a voice in their own path of recovery. If someone is struggling with significant mental health issues, and perhaps cannot make a sound decision on their own, a mental health professional may need to evaluate the survivor and develop a treatment plan.

The National Alliance on Mental Illness (NAMI) lists various mental health professions and their required education as well as their scope of practice:[2]

Psychologists

Psychologists hold a doctoral degree in clinical psychology or another specialty such as counseling or education. They are trained to evaluate a person's mental health using clinical interviews, psychological evaluations, and testing. They can make diagnoses and provide individual and group therapy. Some may have training in specific forms of therapy such as cognitive behavioral therapy (CBT), dialectical behavior therapy (DBT), and other behavioral therapy interventions.

Counselors, Clinicians, Therapists

These masters-level health care professionals are trained to evaluate a person's mental health and use therapeutic techniques based on specific training programs. They operate under a variety of job titles—including counselor, clinician, therapist, or something else—based on the treatment setting. Working with one of these mental health professionals can lead not only to symptom reduction but to better ways of thinking, feeling, and living.

Examples of licensure include:

- LPC, Licensed Professional Counselor
- LMFT, Licensed Marriage and Family Therapist
- LCADAC, Licensed Clinical Alcohol and Drug Abuse Counselor

Clinical Social Workers

Clinical social workers are trained to evaluate a person's mental health and use therapeutic techniques based on specific training programs. They are also trained in case management and advocacy services.

Examples of licensure include:

- LICSW, Licensed Independent Clinical Social Worker
- LCSW, Licensed Clinical Social Worker
- ACSW, Academy of Certified Social Workers

The following two types of health care professionals can prescribe medication. They may also offer assessments, diagnoses, and therapy.

Psychiatrists

Psychiatrists are licensed medical doctors who have completed psychiatric training or medical training about mental health conditions. They can prescribe and monitor medications, and provide therapy. Some have completed additional training in child and adolescent mental health, substance use disorders, or geriatric psychiatry.

Psychiatric or Mental Health Nurse Practitioners (This is the program I am pursuing; I'm hoping to get board certified as a PMHNP.)

Psychiatric mental health nurse practitioners can provide assessment, diagnosis, and therapy for mental health conditions or substance use disorders. In some states, they are also qualified to prescribe and monitor medications. Requirements also vary by state as to the degree of supervision necessary by a licensed psychiatrist.

- NCLEX, National Council Licensure Examination
- PMHNP-BC, Board Certification in psychiatric nursing through the American Academy of Nurses Credentialing Center

Pastoral Counseling

The American Association of Pastoral Counselors requires their students to hold both bachelor's and master's degrees and theological training before they are accepted. If someone says they want counseling from only a Christian perspective, this option is the most widely recognized as professional, as it holds to strict standards.

Other types of counselors can be social workers or certified peer counselors. The Stephen Ministry is a common lay-counseling ministry option, but it does not require the same level of education and training (and accountability) as licensed professionals who are background-checked through the FBI before they can sit for their board exams.

Inpatient Treatment

Inpatient or residential treatment is when a survivor goes to a psychiatric facility (usually not the stereotypical "psych wards" of movies). Most are actually like hotels with serene environments. I have been to two residential facilities. Both have trauma-specific tracks and medication management. Inpatient facilities are unique in the sense that patients spend all day in a variety of therapies (talk, group, recreational, body work such as trauma-informed massage or yoga—which helps survivors reconnect with their bodies—animal or equine therapy, and nutritional therapy, all of which have evidence-based benefits). Some intensives are a week long, and others are indefinite. If someone has (or can raise) the funds to go, it's a worthwhile investment.

If you are supporting someone who has been abused, and could perhaps benefit from an intensive professional therapy, know that in some cases, professional help may be hard to find and, in the US, it can be expensive. This should not be a deterrent to seeking care, but knowing these things in advance can help you and the survivor come up with a plan so that the survivor does not feel immediately defeated or overwhelmed when considering it.

For example, I see a certified trauma counselor who is licensed. Her fee is $100 per session. I also see a PMHNP for some psychotherapy and medication management, and that is $150 per session. My monthly medication cost ranges from $55–$505, depending on the month. Insurance reimburses me for about 25 to 30 percent. Inpatient therapy is not usually covered, although more are beginning to accept insurance reimbursement. Some websites, such as talkspace.com or Teladoc, offer relatively inexpensive and convenient options if local help isn't available or affordable. Some employers may also offer Employee Assistance Programs (EAP) at no cost or at a nominal fee, so it is worth looking into those options if they are available. If someone has insurance, they can often get a list of in-network providers and a full explanation of the benefits they have.

In severe cases, a survivor may need to go on disability for a season, or perhaps permanently, because of his or her mental health. There is a stigma around receiving disability benefits, but they can be life-saving for those who are suffering, offering a way to pay for basic needs and sometimes health insurance when a survivor is not able to work. I was diagnosed with complex PTSD at the first inpatient facility I went to and had to receive disability benefits for several months when I was unable to work. Receiving a clinical diagnosis from a medical professional is the first step in applying for disability benefits. Once the survivor is able to work again, the program allows for a progressive reentry back into the workplace, just in case the survivor is not as mentally or physically ready as originally anticipated.

It's important to be direct and specific when asking mental health professionals about their specialty and previous work. Have they worked with sexual assault victims? Have they had training related to treating trauma? If the therapist and survivor don't mesh well or the survivor feels unsafe, are there other counselors he or she could recommend? Where does the counseling take place, and does the survivor feel safe in that location? Believe it or not, there are counselors who will meet you in your home, as often people feel safest there.

Finally, be sure to check reviews on Yelp, Google, NextDoor, and Facebook too. Do your homework, and don't just trust one source for reviews, but it's helpful to just get an idea of what people are saying. You can generally check with the accrediting or licensing board to see whether they have ever had their license removed or suspended for any reason. Keep in mind that while diplomas, degrees, and certifications are proof of education, they do not always mean someone is experienced or compassionate.

Being Strong Enough to
Carry: Staying Healthy

When you choose to walk alongside a survivor, you're taking on a very worthy but extremely difficult task. Yes, it *is* a burden. You are choosing to help carry someone's weight—and that can affect you spiritually, emotionally, and sometimes physically. Remember, we don't need to be perfect in order to help someone, but we do need to be healthy.

To keep yourself healthy as you embark on this journey, it's important to take time to care for yourself in the same ways you're encouraging someone else to. Here are some specific ways to care for yourself as you support others.

YOUR BRAIN

It's easy (and wise) to pick up a few books on understanding trauma and abuse. But don't overdo it. You don't want to overimmerse your entire mind in learning about trauma without enough mental breaks to help sustain your burden or interest in it. As someone who is studying this stuff full-time right now, I can tell you that reading the never-ending studies and therapies in a thirst for knowledge can become a black hole of fascination. To keep myself sane, I pick up a couple of light-on-the-brain magazines when I go to the grocery store. Sometimes it's a good escape to spend your mental time with things that aren't so serious, such as the royal family drama, Hollywood love triangles (remember, this book is a judgment-free zone), or guides such as *50 Ways to Keep Your Preschooler's Room Clean* and *I Love Broccoli: A Toddler's Obsession with Cruciferous Vegetables.** Whatever break your mind

---

* Clearly these are fictional works. But please send all relevant parenting tips to me via the contact form on my website.

needs, take it. Diversity will help keep you creative and sharp without getting too nerdy about brainy things.

YOUR BODY

Keeping in physical shape is only going to help you serve better. It's tempting to indulge in *treat-yo'-self* a little more when we are under stress (which you will be), so keep your body as healthy as you can with nutritious food, lots of water, exercise, and plenty of sleep. It will be challenging, so if you know this when you enter the journey, you can prevent lethargy, burnout, and overindulgence from creeping into your life.

YOUR MIND

Keep in mind that counseling is good for *you* too. It may be helpful for those who are caring for sexual abuse survivors to have their own outlet to talk and share how they are doing. In a counseling relationship, you can share more specifically about how you're emotionally handling this season. Be careful not to turn your counseling into a way to get advice for how to help. Instead, focus on *you* and things you can do to stay emotionally healthy. It's extremely hard to process the evils of sexual abuse, and the darkness of it may become overwhelming. Actually, it *will* be overwhelming. Whatever tools you can use to stay emotionally healthy, use them all.

YOUR HEART

Since you are helping to carry another's burden, you are going to need someone outside the situation to help you. This need not only be a professional counselor. It can be a trusted friend, a safe person you can vent to, cry with, share with, and ask advice from. You don't have to (and probably shouldn't) disclose whom you are helping or specifics of the event, but it's important for you to unload some of the weight. What are some ways you refresh yourself? Are you introverted or extroverted? Does having coffee with a friend fill you, or do you decompress by yourself before you meet up with friends? Know your rhythms and respect them well. If you find yourself getting burned out, evaluate why, and reach out for help. Make sure you don't become disconnected from your community in the process of helping someone else find theirs.

And even though I've already mentioned caring for your body, remember that incorporating exercise is a great way to stay emotionally fit too. Your body produces feel-good chemicals such as dopamine and beta-endorphins, which are chemicals that have some structural similarities to morphine. The discipline of exercise can help you process some of the pain you may feel from helping a survivor. That's right—working out can help you process your own emotions!

YOUR EMOTIONS

Did you know we're wired with something dubbed "mirror neurons"?[3] Our neurons reflect and internally process the pain (or joy, or nervousness—almost any emotion) that we see in someone else. This is what allows us to have empathy. We reflect the emotions of another person into our body and imagine, *What if I were going through that?* Mirror neurons can be a source of great compassion and introspection. But they can also provoke anxiety.

Think about reading a story about someone going through a horrific experience. You don't know the person. It may be something on the news or an article you found on a Facebook rabbit trail. Your brain thinks—very rapidly—what it would be like to go through that, and depending on how your neurons work, your body can go through a moment of similar trauma response. In a healthy scenario, your brain and body will know quickly that you are not in harm's way, and your vicarious scenario will pass quickly.

But when you're constantly helping someone who has experienced trauma, these neurons will light up a lot more frequently. This can unintentionally cause you to experience something called "trauma by proxy," "secondary trauma," or "vicarious trauma." It can have devastating results if it's not dealt with early on. Knowing that this can happen (especially the more empathetic you are) means that it's essential for you to get ahead of it. Make sure you have a positive support system and, if possible, a counselor who knows about trauma. Something as simple as keeping an affirmation of truth ("You are safe," etc.) where you can regularly see it can be a good reminder that you are, in fact, safe.

YOUR SPIRIT

If you are a Christian (or if, by chance, you picked this book up and are a part of a different spiritual community), don't neglect your spiritual needs. Make sure you are diving deep into Scripture and plugging in to your church community, letting them know that you are helping someone who's going through a difficult time. When I was in my twenties and was carrying a very heavy load as a church staff member, a pastor saw me burning out and asked me, "Is serving the church interfering with your communion with Christ?" It was a perspective-shifting question. If you're not a Christian and you consider yourself spiritual, do what you need to do in order to stay connected to your spirit. That might mean spending additional time with other people, getting out to explore nature, or listening to music. People express their spirituality—Christian or otherwise—in a variety of ways. Just make sure you aren't neglecting this aspect of who you are.

Is serving the church interfering with your communion with Christ?

Finally, if helping someone begins to take too heavy a toll on your life and ends up destroying your relationships, it may not be the best season for you to carry this weight. If that's the case, be honest with the survivor, and find ways to enlist the help of other people. This doesn't mean you must stop being involved, but it may be a time to step back and help in a smaller way. Remember, no one "fixes" a survivor—it takes a community of love, care, and acceptance to experience healing together. You don't have to be that whole village. But you can play a small part, and the part you play still makes a big difference.

—

We are all called to help survivors in some way. Start by getting to know the survivors around you. Are there any survivors in your committed or vulnerable categories of relationships? Are you a pastor or church leader who can help survivors who attend your church?

Have you considered how your church might assist survivors in getting the help they need and taking a step toward rebuilding trust within the church community?

Are you a professional counselor who can offer your services or partner with a church and guide them in helping?

Are there safe, physical spaces in your organization or community that could be beneficial for groups for survivors and supporters—a comforting room where they could meet? Are there other trainings or seminars you could host?

Think about the relationships in your life, and brainstorm different roles you could take to help others.

How will *you* answer the call to help survivors?

Chapter 6

Helping Survivors: A Practical Guide

*I*f you've picked up this book, you likely know someone who's been affected by sexual abuse and you're looking to understand and to help them. In all the polling I've conducted over the years, 100 percent of respondents personally knew someone who was abused.

But if you don't personally know someone affected, I'm grateful that you are reading this proactively. Regardless of your experience or familiarity with this topic, it's wonderful that you are taking the time to learn more about abuse, to understand the effects of trauma, and to determine what is needed to have a response plan in place. Your efforts will help to support survivors and avoid causing additional pain. Having a plan allows us to create some emotional margin and saves us time by knowing what steps we need to take *before* we need to take them.

If you are a survivor, reading through this chapter may give you some ideas on how to communicate with those who want to support you, as well as some help in talking with other survivors. On one hand, you may read certain parts and think, "Oh my goodness! This is totally me!" and on the other hand, there may be ideas or suggestions that do not resonate with you at all. Whether or not you relate fully with all the ideas in this chapter, know that your experience—whatever the specifics—is valid and that you are not abnormal or beyond help.

The Three Cs of Responding to an Abuse Crisis

In nursing school, we were given tons of information. And we were expected to remember this information in stressful, life-threatening situations. Even the most basic first aid and CPR—things we practice and are trained on every year—can be easily forgotten when you are called to jump in and help on a "code blue" (when someone goes into cardiac arrest or stops breathing) or even when you're off the clock and there is an emergency. To help us remember, almost everything we learn is memorized using some sort of alliteration or mnemonic device. For example, if someone may have had a stroke, all we need to remember is to "Act *FAST*." The letters of the word FAST all stand for a different concept to consider in evaluating whether a stroke has occurred—Face, Arms, Speech, Time. Instead of wracking our brain trying to remember every

The Three Cs: check, call, and care.

detail—What are the symptoms of a stroke? What do I need to do?—we only need to remember the acronym.

Some of the mnemonics are corny (and others are rather vulgar), but regardless, they're effective. So to help you remember how to respond to someone in an abuse crisis situation, I've come up with an alliteration that should make your response a little easier to remember. I call them the Three Cs: check, call, and care.

CHECK

The first *C* is *check*. This is a reminder to assess the safety and well-being of the survivor. While this is especially important in cases of sexual or physical abuse, it doesn't apply only there. Make it your first priority to check with the person to make sure they are safe and okay. Here are some questions you might ask yourself (or the victim) when you are checking to see whether they are safe. Depending on the answer, you can decide whether they need to be moved into a safer place or perhaps they just need someone to sit with them for a time.

- Is the person facing any physical threat or other type of threat?
- Did the abuse just occur?
- Is the person a threat to themselves or to others—either suicidal or having thoughts of harming themselves or anyone else?
- Is the person experiencing any medical emergencies?
- Is the person experiencing any emotional emergencies (shock, a nervous breakdown, uncontrollable emotions such as anger, sadness, grief, or anxiety)?

- If the person has children or others in their care (including pets), do arrangements need to be made to ensure their safety and well-being?

If the person who has come to you is in danger of harming themselves, harming others, or being harmed, you need to take action. Don't take no for an answer. Remove them from whatever threat they're facing. Do not take this situation lightly, even if they are just joking around or are trying to reassure you that they're fine. Take them to the nearest emergency room or police station to get additional help. If they won't go, or even if they make *you* go, call 911 and send help to them.

Also know that as you try this, the person may (and likely will) get upset at you and even threaten to end your relationship. That's okay, and it's a normal response. I had to take a suicidal friend of mine to an emergency room, and he swore he'd never speak to me again. But I knew I'd rather have him alive and not speaking to me than harmed or dead. Your friend's life is worth saving, no matter what consequences may follow.

Your friend's life is worth saving, no matter what consequences may follow.

Secondary to the survivor's well-being is ensuring that the people (or even animals) in their care are also taken care of. When I reported my abuse, I could not have predicted the amount of emotional grief that followed. Even though it was over two decades after it had occurred, the symptoms of physical and emotional trauma flooded me. My husband had to take off from work, and my mom practically lived at our house while caring for our daughter, Charlotte. I needed help and was unable to provide adequate childcare by myself during that time.

Regardless of when the abuse happened, understand that a survivor can experience a powerful emotional crisis at any time. Your first priority is to *check* and make sure that immediate needs are met and that they are in a safe place.

CALL

After you've checked for the well-being of the survivor, the next step, if necessary, is to *call the authorities*. If you've checked on a friend or loved one and all is well, wonderful. But if you become aware of *any* abuse of anyone, contact law enforcement (and do anything you can to ensure that the survivor—child or adult—is placed in safe care immediately). If you suspect abuse and you don't think the person is in immediate danger, you can report the suspicion to law enforcement. Most states have a way of reporting online. You can usually report abuse anonymously, but if you do use your name, the law protects you from being sued, as long as you report in good faith and not maliciously or falsely.

What do you do when an adult shares with you that they were abused earlier in life?

An adult has just shared with you that they were abused as a child. Legally, this is something of a gray area. Are you mandated to report the abuse to authorities? *Maybe.* If the abuser is still at large and could be hurting other people, you should *always* report it. If you make a report in good faith, the law still protects you from being sued.

My own story can be helpful in understanding what to do in this situation. When I reported my abuse to the organization where my abuser worked, I was twenty-five years old. Because I was an adult when I came forward, they were not legally obligated to report the abuse. But because Mark was likely still working with and had access to children at the time, they *should* have reported it. There are no severe criminal or civil repercussions for corporate or nonprofit entities choosing not to report, and, at the time, there were no consequences for not reporting this within their own denomination. But that is changing.

As I consider it now, several years later, I wish that the organization would have reported my abuse, or encouraged me to, and then walked with me through the criminal process even though at the time, I didn't think I could handle it. Thankfully, we can learn from the mistakes of the past and continue to do what's good and right and true. For the sake of those you love, and all those who might be helped by their coming forward, do not ignore red flags, and always consider reporting the abuse to authorities when you can.

What if the survivor doesn't want to report?

If you are told about an abusive situation that is within the confines of mandatory reporting (i.e., a child or minor), you don't have a choice—you must report. But in circumstances that fall outside a legal obligation, where the survivor is an adult *and* the person who abused them is not placing anyone in danger, it is always best to respect the survivor's wishes.

In addition to reporting to law enforcement, it's often a good idea to bring other trusted people into the situation with the survivor's permission and help. Ask the survivor what he or she thinks and who they trust and would like to have supporting them. Does the survivor need help telling a spouse or other family members? Would bringing in a pastor or a counselor help? Is this a situation that needs civil litigation?

Ultimately, the story of abuse belongs to the survivor, and they may make it clear that only you are to know their story. Or they may feel as though they need to go public with what is happening. Or perhaps they want to share this within a group of friends. There is no wrong way for a survivor to talk about their abuse. Help them, encourage them, and most importantly, listen to them. When necessary or desired, make the phone call that is needed.

CARE

The third *C* is *care.* Care for survivors extends beyond simply checking on their safety in a certain moment or making a phone call. It is a long-term commitment. I wish I could give you an easy list of things you should do to care for a survivor, but the truth is that it varies greatly from person to person based on the trauma, the person, your gifts, your relationship, and their need. What I outline here are some general suggestions that may not apply to every abuse situation, but I hope these ideas give you a few specific ways of helping, and hopefully they spark some additional ideas that you can do to serve a loved one in your life who has faced abuse.

When you take on the role of caring, it's easy to fall into a default role because of how you're naturally wired. Here are a few roles that people may "naturally" assume. Staying within the strict boundaries of what *you* think is best won't serve the survivor (and even yourself) in the best possible way. As you read through this section, see if you tend to gravitate toward one or more of these roles in your care for survivors.

Fix it and forget it: When they see something wrong, they want to fix it. They want healing to fall into a linear space. If someone is sad, they want to make them happy. If someone needs money, they help them out. If *X*, then *Y*. Problem solved. Let's move on.

If this is your tendency, please remember that healing is not linear. One doesn't just "move on" from abuse. Survivors are not projects with problems that need to be fixed. My friend and fellow survivor Megan Lively once drew a picture of what recovery looks like, and it was full of peaks and valleys. Survivors will never, ever forget what has happened to them, and they will go through various ups and downs in their journeys in processing their experiences.

The savior: When someone acts as a savior, their role in the healing process is inflated and sometimes "greater" than that of the survivor. Because they haven't experienced the pain of abuse, they mistakenly (and sometimes unwittingly) believe they are more godly or even emotionally stronger than others. Saviors see their suggestions as the best and sometimes the *only* way of healing, and they are easily offended when survivors don't share their views. In extreme cases, saviors can become martyrs, looking for recognition for how wonderful they are as they reach down into the pit of despair to help the broken. If you notice these tendencies as you support someone, take a step back and check in with the person or people you are helping. Listen to them, to their wishes and needs, and realize it is *their* healing that *you* are there to help.

The avenger: Avengers see injustice in abuse, and they get angry. They think that whoever hurt the person they love should pay, and they come up with strategies to right the wrongs that have happened on their watch. Abuse is a great evil, and we do need to seek justice, but justice is not the sole focus of our support, nor is it always the primary goal in the relationship. Even though the avenger's intentions are good in seeking reconciliation for a survivor, it's easy for them to lose the forest for the trees—neglecting the daily needs of the survivor in a blind pursuit of justice. Similar to the savior tendency, taking a step back and reconnecting with the heart of the survivor is key here. You can't let the cause overshadow the needs of the person right in front of you.

The overspiritualizer: Sharing Scripture and offering prayers are helpful and sometimes welcome. But taken to the extreme, overspiritualizing can be damaging to a survivor's spirit. When I was contemplating suicide, curled up in a ball in my bed, no Bible verse or prayer was going to help me in that moment. When you force God on a survivor before they are ready or emphasize that God is the only way they will ever find peace again, this can risk being dismissive of their pain. It may also reinforce the perceived chasm they feel between themselves and God. God can feel absent in our trauma and grief. There is a time to lament—to cry out in honesty that God feels far away. And there's a time to remind people that God is near to the brokenhearted. Be aware of the time or phase the survivor is in, and let them stay there for now, knowing that our help ultimately comes from the Lord, yes, but that help will be received when a survivor is ready to seek it. Don't assume the person needs a come-to-Jesus moment or try to push your own timeline. That distressed wood sign with Romans 8:28 painted on it or tagging them in the Bible

> *When I was contemplating suicide, no Bible verse or prayer was going to help me.*

Verse of the Day Instagram posts isn't going to save them. In some cases, these things will only further isolate them from your support.

The expert: Sometimes people are equipped with knowledge. Experts think they know everything about trauma and abuse and healing. They offer support from a cognitive or academic level, and while it's important to understand what survivors are going through and that information may be helpful to survivors as they heal, coming off as the expert furthers feelings of inadequacy and may invalidate how the survivor feels. Why? Often survivors hear the "expert" reminding them that what they are going through is typical, textbook material, nothing special. Knowledge is power, but know-it-alls are off-putting, especially for a survivor who is trying to make sense of their new normal. It's essential to realize that although you may understand on one level what's going on, you cannot feel the deep emotions or consequences felt by the survivor. Until you are able to help grieve with a person on a heart-level, helping them on an intellectual level isn't possible—or helpful.

The ghost: Ghosts have good intentions. They read this book and every other book and believe they are ready to help survivors. They are there at the beginning, but then at some point they realize they're in over their heads (which is totally fine!). When this happens, instead of telling survivors that they need space or that they need help, and instead of just being honest, they simply disappear. If you want to or tend to become a ghost, remember that survivors often fear abandonment because of their (wrong) belief that they're not worthy of relationships. When a ghost vanishes, that belief is reinforced. If you find yourself becoming a ghost, remember that it's okay if you need to step out of the survivor's healing process for any reason, for any length of time, but it's really important to simply communicate that. It may be hard for a survivor to understand, but it's even more painful for a survivor to think they did something wrong and drove you away.

Caring for the Body, Heart, Mind, and Spirit

Trauma affects people's bodies, minds, hearts, and spirits. Using each of these areas as a paradigm for holistic health and healing, I'll provide some practical advice on how to support a survivor. Remember each situation is unique, so use wisdom and discernment in applying these suggestions.

BODY

The body of a survivor suffers great harm. It was the body that was violated first. It may have been beaten, penetrated, or violated in some way. In any case, another person took what God created for his good and his glory and tarnished it with evil. God does not hold the survivor responsible for what happened to their body, and he sees him or her as pure. He grieves over the pain that was caused.

DISCONNECTION

To survive the abuse physically and emotionally, survivors often disassociate or disconnect from sensations in their bodies. For survivors, being mindful and present in our bodies after abuse has occurred is a difficult task and can cause anxiety.

Reconnecting with our bodies requires a lot of hard work, and usually professional help.

As you sit with a survivor, if they're experiencing some intense emotions, you can ask them to describe what they feel. When I get anxious, I've learned to notice that I feel a tightness in my chest and a pounding in my stomach. When I'm angry, I feel hot and rushed. When I'm sad, my body feels tired. It may not seem to have any immediate benefits, but asking a survivor to recognize what their body is experiencing allows us to start reconnecting our mind and our body together when we've tried to keep them separated for so long.

BODY IMAGE AND HARM

When the body has been abused, a survivor will frequently see it as broken. Many survivors turn to overeating or wearing baggy clothes in an attempt to blend in and avoid future abuse. *If nobody finds me attractive, nobody will take advantage of me.* Others may act on the opposite end of the spectrum and be obsessed with image so that they feel as though they're in control, or they want to make sense of the belief that it was their fault that the abuse happened. Some engage in self-harm, punishing their body or hurting it in some way. The physical pain can be so sharp that it distracts from the emotional pain, for a moment anyway.

If you see a survivor mistreating their body, gently engage them if you have a history of relational trust built with them. If they've opened up to you about this, you can ask them to help you understand. Make sure you let them know that you are not judging them and that you certainly don't see them any differently. Tell them you love them, and show them you love them, no matter what.

APPROPRIATE PHYSICAL TOUCH AND SPACE

When my husband comes home, I often hear the garage door open and close and then hear him come through the back door. Even though I hear him and know he will be entering the space I am in, if I don't *see* him come up behind me to give me a hug, I jump, and I get upset. I feel uncomfortable when men give me hugs, and I don't like people getting too physically close to me.

Many survivors don't like physical touch, and this is something you need to be keenly aware of. You may love hugs, high fives, or a supportive touch on an arm or a hand. But when you're helping a survivor, please ask "Is it okay if I give you a hug?" or "I would really like to offer you some comfort. Please feel free to say no, but can I hold your hand while you're telling me this?" You may feel awkward doing so, but your courtesy and respecting his or her physical boundaries will be a welcome act.

EXERCISE AND EATING WELL

Just as you need to care for your body as you help us, you can encourage us to care for our bodies. Not only does exercise and eating well nourish us and help us be physically healthy, it also helps us emotionally. Something as simple as going on a walk with us or heading to a park in the sunshine will help us feel better. Be patient with us. It can take a lot of effort for us to regain the confidence to use our bodies for good and to get moving again.

AN AWKWARD BUT NECESSARY
DIALOGUE ABOUT VIRGINITY

When a survivor was forced to have intercourse and was a virgin prior to abuse, they may wonder whether they're still a virgin. In the anatomical sense of the word, they cannot undo what was done. But I believe that, spiritually speaking, our Creator supersedes biological terminology. He created us. *He* defines our identity.

In Christianity, we have made such a big deal about maintaining our virginity until we are married. In our fight for purity, however, we have reduced the complexity and mystery that is happening in sex to a physical transaction. The idea of "losing one's virginity" has become so focused on the act of physical penetration that we forget it is also more than that.

Sex is something that affects not only the body but the mind and spirit too.

Sex is something that affects not only the body but the mind and spirit too. When supporting a survivor after something as horrible as sexual assault, you can encourage your friend that they bear no weight of the crime committed against them. Before God, they are as pure as before the assault.

MIND AND EMOTIONS

After abuse, a survivor may have a difficult time understanding the truth about who they are and whether they can trust their feelings. Because of the nature of sexual abuse, they may believe they are at fault, that they're responsible, or that healing is impossible.

EMOTIONAL ROLLER COASTERS

It's normal for a survivor to experience a myriad of emotions and to experience them deeply. Feelings that will commonly surface are shame, guilt, fear, panic, anger, and despair. My husband, Tim, has said that in my least healthy times, he feels as if he has to walk on eggshells because he's not sure what I'm feeling or what I might project. We've had to work on our communication. He tries to be intentional in asking me what I'm feeling and why, and whether he can help relieve it in any way. I try to be open and honest about how and what I'm feeling. I may be experiencing a great deal of anger after reading a news story about an abuser who did not receive the proper consequence for his actions. I may be anxious because I saw something that reminds me of my own abuse story. I may feel guilty that I am not as close with Tim as I think (or I think *he thinks*) I should be.

It can be hard not to take a survivor's emotions personally. More likely than not, the survivor is having a difficult time communicating his or her feelings because they are afraid you'll judge them, leave them, or consider them unjustified in having these emotions. Survivors may be embarrassed for feeling the way they do. In the church, we're often tempted to wear the "I'm fine" mask, and when we're not fine, it's unbelievably exhausting to try and pretend. We also see everyone else feeling fine (or wearing their "I'm fine" masks) and feel horribly left out and disconnected from others.

Reassurance that you're with us regardless of our emotional struggles is important and will help us tremendously. If you see that we're spending an unhealthy amount of time in one emotional state (angry all the time, sad all the time, guilty all the time), gently ask us how we are doing (please don't assume) and whether we need any help.

TRUSTING OURSELVES

Another area where survivors struggle is in trusting ourselves. Even though I was a teenage child when my abuse happened,

I believed I could read people fairly well. Learning that I was fooled has led to significant self-doubt. When we don't trust ourselves, we can be extremely indecisive. Seemingly basic choices such as where to eat or what movie to see can cause us such distress because we fear picking the wrong one. Bigger life decisions, such as careers, relationships, and finances, can be challenging too. You're probably seeing a theme here, but just asking us where we need help is a good way to support us. Walk us through pros and cons, and affirm our steps to make decisions, and that will help us regain confidence.

CONFIDENCE

Abuse renders many survivors incredibly insecure. A combination of shame, unworthiness, and hopelessness leads us to lack confidence in ourselves. It's difficult to believe we're capable of experiencing any good in our lives because of the bad things we've faced. We're waiting for the other shoe to drop, so to speak, so investing in ourselves only to be let down again seems like an insane choice.

People often tell me how much they love my husband. "Oh, he's so funny!" "He's such a hard worker." "He's so creative!" I love going to a work party with him because people just rave about what a brilliant person he is. But when I tell him what people have told me, he's always shocked. Why? Because no one ever tells him these things directly. For whatever reason, we often overlook sharing praise with others, and we become really good at secondhand compliments. If you see something good in a survivor, tell *them*. (I think this is a life lesson for all of us, really.) Helping us regain confidence in any area of our lives is really meaningful to us.

HEART: RELATIONSHIPS

Relationships can be a struggle for survivors. We fear intimacy (both emotional and physical). It's hard for us to trust others. We don't feel as though we're ever at home.

Survivors are often abused within a formative, trusted relationship. It may have been a parent, a pastor or priest, a family member, a friend, a neighbor, a coach, or a teacher—often the survivor knew the person who harmed them. Because of this, it's easy for us to feel as if the abuse is going to happen again, so we build up walls to keep people out. That's how we feel safe.

I read something (and for the life of me I can't seem to find the original source) about how people who are abused move around from place to place frequently. This transient lifestyle is common for two reasons. First, survivors, like me, tend to be naturally afraid as we begin getting to know others. And as people get to know us on a deeper level, we are immediately reminded of the abusive relationship—that person who once knew me well and hurt me. Naturally, we want to move on. Second, the idea of "home"—a safe place where we can't be violated—no longer exists for many survivors. It feels uncomfortable to settle into trusted relationships again, and because it feels foreign to us, we move on.

Earlier, I mentioned that my dad was a pastor. We moved around a few times when I was young—maybe every three years or so. As an adult, I have moved thirty-three times, lived in eight states, and I've attended six colleges or universities. I have held a variety of jobs: a barista, book store manager, graphic designer, administrative assistant, church communications director, band manager and booking agent, author and speaker, editor, and now I work in nursing and patient care. Like many abuse survivors, I'm searching for that safe place to call home, but when I get to that place and "home" starts becoming a reality for me, it's terrifying, and so I move on.

Now that I recognize this, I'm working really, really hard to *stay*. That may involve staying in one place geographically and in my career, but it also means staying *relationally*. I'm fighting to grow deeper in the relationships I have, to initiate new relationships, and to commit to helping others by serving in my community.

If you know survivors and they seem a little hesitant to commit or they're always changing jobs or moving, know that this is common among those who are victims of abuse. Maintaining your commitment to that person and slowly showing them that they can safely be with you helps them overcome their fear.

SPIRIT

Survivors often feel as though God has betrayed them. I know I often struggle with this thought, asking questions such as: Why did God let this happen? Sometimes questions such as this flood my mind and heart. I put up a wall between me and God because I feel that, much like my relationships with people, I can't trust God.

Avoid the tendency to overspiritualize things as you support survivors. There are no easy answers—maybe no answers at all—for those age-old questions we ask regarding the sovereignty of God. It's hard to trust and understand, and survivors may question God's faithfulness and protection. They may even feel guilty about not trusting God or not believing he loves us the way he says he does.

Know that when it comes to answering the "why" behind their abuse, survivors have heard enough of the "God gives us free will" and "evil will always happen in this fallen world" platitudes. So instead of throwing out quick-fix-it phrases, try simply sitting with the person and listening to them. If a survivor wants to go to church, go with them and help them feel safe there. If someone doesn't want to go, please don't force the issue.

I think one of the ways we see God's faithfulness is when we see how he has been faithful in another person's suffering. And the only way this can happen is if others willingly open up and share about their suffering, their secrets, and their dark nights. It's not easy to open the door to that closet where your skeletons and trauma live, but I believe that God makes himself known through how he mends our brokenness.

There's a Japanese art called *kintsugi* that has gained popularity recently. A piece of pottery is broken and put back together, with lacquer and gold filling in the cracks. No pot breaks the same way, so every piece looks different. And because they're put back together with gold, they're

> *There are no easy answers for those age-old questions regarding the sovereignty of God.*

even more beautiful and more valuable than they were before the breaking. As we see how beautifully God has restored broken things around us, as we start to see the way God has mended the wounds of others and how valuable he considers their story, we start to open up to the possibility of our own healing.

The Other Side of the Wall

Much of this book was written in a local coffee shop. It has only a few outlets, and they are hunted like prey in this highly-caffeinated wild. As my laptop battery was fading, a man abandoned his table, and I jumped on it quickly, making an off-the-cuff remark about my luck to someone sitting at the other table by a plug.

Noticing my stack of books, some brightly colored with the word *sex* highlighted on their covers (#awkward), a man at the table asked whether I was in school. We eventually got into a conversation about this book and friendships and faith. It turned out he was a pastor of a nearby Presbyterian church.

As I shared how difficult it is to have community and how hard it is to trust God—that I've built up this huge wall and I never think it's going to come down—he put on his pastor hat and jumped right to the story of the wall of Jericho. "Nobody had to break the wall down," he told me. "Nobody climbed it or attacked it to destroy it. People surrounded the city and walked around the wall. That's how it fell down. It was brought down by the power of God as a community surrounded it."

Think about that again: *the power of God as a community surrounded it.* That's what brought the wall down.

The truth is that most survivors have huge walls built up around them. Nobody really knows how to get in, and lots of people try hammering, calling us to come out, asking us to unlock the doors. But we can't. It's our home and we're frozen. It's the only place we feel safe. We know we're trapped in there with all our baggage and the things we feel that we're enslaved to. We *want* to experience life with people on the outside, but we . . . just . . . can't.

Supporters are the ones marching outside the walls. They faithfully go around and around and blow the horn, and by the power of God alone—not the strength of the people inside the walls or the people outside them—the walls fall down.

In the story, the Israelites go in and kill off everything and everyone *except* Rahab and those she loves. Rahab was a prostitute and was seen by society as unclean and untouchable. I'm sure she didn't feel so awesome about herself either. And like Rahab, survivors feel "unclean." But I'm encouraged to know that that God *wants* to send a community after me and that he *wants* to pursue me. He values the woman behind the wall.

I'm encouraged to know that that God wants to send a community after me.

What's the role of survivors in the process? It's to be obedient to him and to stay committed to their loved one on the other side of the wall. Just stay. Keep circling the wall. Keep showing up. And eventually God will do what God does. Maybe he will chip away at it bit by bit, or maybe he will bring the whole thing down in one fell swoop, but either way, that wall will come down, and the survivor inside will know they're free.

The Six Bs
and One Please Don't

Knowing what to do when someone shares their abuse with you—past or present—can be overwhelming. It's hard to know what to do in the moment of crisis and on the long path to healing. Here are six quick (and again alliterated!) reminders of what to do and what not to do as we wrap up this chapter.

Be-lieve: Believe the survivor. Now is not the time to find out all the details and determine whether the person is being truthful or not. Very few survivors share their stories to begin with, and those who do are highly unlikely, statistically speaking, to make up the abuse or to embellish it. This is doubly true when it comes to children, as children don't have the "carnal knowledge" (as the law defines it) or capacity to lie about such horrible acts. Believe the person, and let them know you believe them.

Be There: Be physically present if you can. *Compassion* means "to suffer with."[1] It is an active term, not necessarily just a quality to have.

Be Aware: Look out for the survivor's safety and emotional well-being. Are they in any danger? Do you see anything that indicates they need immediate safety and care? Gently guide them to the hospital, police, or to a safe place.

Be Sensitive: When we hear the horrors of abuse, sometimes it's difficult to control our body language. Make sure you maintain an open stance. Lean in. Arms down. Nod your head "yes" as you listen; don't shake your head "no" at the evil of it, as that can show that you don't believe them.

Be Consistent: As I mentioned earlier, consistently showing up and following through on what you say you're going to do goes a long way in earning and keeping trust. Consistently check in and help survivors take the next right step, even if that step is resting.

Be Encouraging: Life can seem hopeless to a survivor. It feels as though God has abandoned us and people have betrayed us. We think we're broken. What's there to be hopeful about? Affirm and reaffirm the personhood of the survivor: that he or she is worthy, valuable, made new, safe to share—as well as affirm and reaffirm the nature of God's goodness and faithfulness (when appropriate).

And please don't: Please don't ask for details of the abuse (like what someone was wearing or whether they were drinking or anything that would suggest they are at fault). Don't say how surprised you are because the offender is "such a good guy" or "wow—you never would expect he could do such a thing." Don't overspiritualize or cover our pain with Band-Aid Bible verses. Don't expect (or encourage) a survivor to forgive and forget or move on. Don't share the survivor's story or tell them how they should or shouldn't share their story. Don't betray the survivor's confidence in any way—it's the foundation of trust, and of your relationship with the survivor as you help him or her begin their journey of healing.

Chapter 7

Preventing, Recognizing, and Responding to Childhood Sexual Abuse

*A*buse can happen to people of all ages, but those who are most vulnerable to being abused are children. Every nine minutes, Child Protective Services finds evidence for a claim of child abuse, and that includes only *reported* abuse.[1] Due to access, physical size, and power differentials, children are inherently easier targets for perpetrators. In this chapter, we'll look at what we can do to prevent child abuse in our families, churches, and other organizations. What do you do when a child confesses he or she was sexually abused? What are some precautions we can take? What are the signs that a child has been abused?

As a parent, this topic provokes much anxiety in me. I never knew the love I could have for a person until the moment I knew

I was pregnant, and that love has grown even more as my daughter, Charlotte, develops into the beautiful girl she is becoming. I cannot fathom how anyone would see the wonderful, innocent, and lovely creation of a child and defile it for his or her own sexual gratification. The thought enrages me. I look back on myself as a child and think of how young and vulnerable I was when I was abused. There is no doubt that sexually abusing a child is evil. If you are the parent of a child who has been abused, I grieve for you and for your child, and I'm both angry and sorry.

Preventing Childhood Sexual Abuse

As Christians who believe sex is a sacred gift from God, we sometimes mistakenly assume that we are divinely protected from sexual abuse. We think that the church—and those within it—are exceptions to the terror that wreaks havoc in the world. That could never happen in our church, we mistakenly assume. Surely there aren't perpetrators here, in our midst. Surely it won't happen to *my* kid.

Unfortunately, we know these assumptions are false. When we look at the American population, 20 to 25 percent of us have been sexually abused as children, and plenty of people in those percentages experienced that abuse in a local church.[*] Thankfully, though, there are some things we can do to protect ourselves.

---

[*] I wrote extensively about child abuse in my book *5 Things Every Parent Needs to Know about Their Kids and Sex*. If you want to learn more about how to talk to your kids about sex (what to talk about and at what age), the media, abuse, and trafficking, that book goes in depth with a lot of research, information about apps, child development, and some theology surrounding sex. You can get it on online or have it ordered to your local bookstore.

Here are several ways you can work to make sure your children are protected from perpetrators.

BEYOND THE BACKGROUND CHECK

Background checks are important, but they aren't everything. For example, at every place of employment Mark (the man who abused me) went to, the organization performed a background check. And every report turned up squeaky clean. This is true for most offenders. The resume (and references) of an abuser when they are moving from job to job are certainly not going to have abuse listed anywhere. A public accusation of sexually abusing a child isn't something one wants to bring up in an interview. On top of this, there are plenty of cases where sexual offenders take plea deals in which, as part of their deal, they are not listed on the state or national sexual offender's registry, or they plea down to lesser crimes that don't seem as serious as a sexual offense. While I wrote this book, Mark accepted a plea deal in which he received deferred adjudication. If he follows the conditions of his probation, he will not have a criminal record or be a registered sex offender. I had the opportunity of being at his sentencing hearing and, as I stood twenty feet away from him, read him a Victim Impact Statement. You can find that statement at annemariemiller.com/statement.

In the American population, 20 to 25 percent of us have been sexually abused as children.

So yes, continue to get background checks if you are hiring a childcare provider in your home or a pastor in your church, but know that it's highly unlikely that something will show up on their background check, even if they are a prior offender. And they certainly won't list an accusation on their job or volunteer application, nor will their references include people who know about the offense. If some of their references do happen to know, they likely won't say anything out of loyalty and solidarity to the offender.

REQUIREMENTS WHEN WORKING WITH CHILDREN

It's important for your church to develop a clear set of requirements for anyone—staff or volunteers—working with children. To get you started with some ideas, I've included an example of what those requirements might look like. Use this as a starting point, but feel free to adapt it to your own context.* The statements are followed by my commentary in *italics*.

- Anyone who will be working with children will be screened for a history of sexually abusing minors or violating the boundaries of minors.

I think the latter part of this requirement is an important step in proactively determining potential risk.

- Anyone working with children should have a completed background check, which includes each state/county that the candidate has resided in for the past seven years and a national sex offender registry check.

---

* Much of this comes from the Conference of Major Superiors of Men (A Jesuit organization that is part of the Catholic Church). They have some excellent requirements and a thorough application process for anyone who wants to work with children. The evangelical church could learn a lot from our Catholic brothers and sisters who have been working on new policies and protocol.

Some criminal offenders, as I've already mentioned, will make deals or plea down to lower charges to avoid jail time. These may not show up on a felony check. Some of these pleas include having to register as a sex offender in lieu of serving time in prison. On the flip side, pleas include jail time but exclude registering as a sex offender.

- Anyone working with children will have a minimum of three documented personal references (including at least one from a family member) and two professional references, for a total of five references.

Interviewing secondhand references, or a reference given by a primary reference, is another way to look for potential concerns. I recommend asking every candidate to sign a disclosure allowing you to ask anybody anything. If they refuse, they're probably hiding something.

- Applicants should have a face-to-face interview and at least two people present for the interview (e.g., church members, elders, parents, etc.).

It's important to look someone in the eyes and be able to hear their voice. Having two people there allows more opportunity for any concerns to be noticed and voiced, as well as witnessed.

- For those in key leadership positions, there may need to be a review of publicly accessible content that mentions the applicant, including a review of available social media, personal blog sites, and websites.

This can take some digging. Find someone who is good at research-
ing online, as there are legal and protected ways to find cached websites
that have been taken down and ways to search usernames that can help
discover someone's online habits.

- Any individual who has an established history of sexually abusing a minor in his past, or who has acquired/intentionally viewed child pornography, will not be permitted to work with children.

While this seems obvious, this is something every organization
should directly ask a ministry candidate who may end up working
with children.

- Ministry leaders should be provided education and training that helps them to identify those who may be at risk of sexually abusing a minor.

Remember, we are biased to think well of those we know or people
who are like us. It helps to provide your leaders with the training they
need to identify the behavior of a perpetrator/abuser.[2]

EDUCATION AND TRAINING

Following this last point above, another way to help prevent child abuse organizationally is to initiate an education for your staff or volunteers, as well as parents and the community. The organization Darkness to Light has evidence-based programs that can help with this. Check around for local ministries and organizations that might be able to help as well.

One of the basic initiatives in Darkness to Light is the *5 Steps to Protecting Our Children.*

1. Learn the Facts

   Educate yourself on the facts about childhood sexual abuse: the statistics, knowing who the predators are, and understanding how survivors react to trauma.

2. Minimize Opportunity

   Eighty percent of incidents happen in isolation. Maintain safe environments by keeping adult/child involvement in groups or always supervised by another adult. An adult and a child rarely need to be alone in an organizational setting.

3. Talk about It

   Talk to kids about sex and their bodies at age-appropriate times. My book *5 Things Every Parent Needs to Know about Their Kids and Sex* has an entire chapter based on the latest psychological and scientific research dedicated to what's appropriate and necessary to talk about at every age. Some parents are concerned that talking about sex can "ruin" a child's innocence. We talk about water safety and fire safety, so thinking about sex and appropriate relationships/physical touch as prevention will both normalize the shame that can surround talking about sex as well as equip our children to recognize unsafe behaviors and people.

4. Recognize the Signs

   Know the signs of childhood sexual abuse. Remember that seeing physical signs is rare, and emotional/

psychological symptoms are most common and vary by age. Also, know the signs that someone could be a perpetrator.

5. React Responsibly

Listen and believe. Don't ask questions that can confuse reality for a child (e.g., asking "Where did he touch you?" instead of "Did he touch your breasts?") This is more appropriate and accurate.[3]

Darkness to Light also has a course (online or in person) that is the only course scientifically proven to "increase knowledge, improve attitudes, and change child protective behaviors"[4] in preventing, recognizing, and responding to abuse. Their website is d2l.org.

Recognizing Childhood Sexual Abuse

The indicators that a child is being sexually abused are usually seen in one of two extremes. In my case, I retreated inward to cope with what was happening. I internalized it and shied away. That's one indicator—a child withdraws in a noticeable way. But not all children will react this way. Sometimes children act out instead.

Keep in mind that a child showing some of the signs I mention doesn't mean they *have* certainly been abused, but it's still something to note. We should always take a close look any time a child changes his or her demeanor and is acting noticeably out of line with his or her personality.

The website Stop It Now! (stopitnow.org) has compiled a

worksheet that's free to download and includes warning signs for children and teens.[5] Some of the warning signs for abuse include a child who:

- Has nightmares or other sleep problems without an explanation
- Seems distracted or distant at odd times
- Has a sudden change in eating habits
- Refuses to eat
- Loses or drastically increases appetite
- Has trouble swallowing
- Experiences sudden mood swings: rage, fear, insecurity, or withdrawal
- Leaves "clues" that seem likely to provoke a discussion about sexual issues
- Writes, draws, plays, or dreams of sexual or frightening images
- Develops a new or unusual fear of certain people or places
- Refuses to talk about a secret shared with an adult or older child
- Talks about a new older friend
- Suddenly has money, toys, or other gifts without reason
- Thinks of self or body as repulsive, dirty, or bad
- Exhibits adultlike sexual behaviors, language, and knowledge
- Shows signs more typical of younger children
- Reverts to younger behavior (e.g., an older child now behaving like a younger child, such as bed-wetting or thumb-sucking)
- Has new words for private body parts

- Resists removing clothes at appropriate times (bath, bed, toileting, diapering)
- Asks other children to behave sexually or to play sexual games
- Mimics adultlike sexual behaviors with toys or stuffed animals
- Has wetting and soiling accidents unrelated to toilet training

There are also some helpful warning signs in older adolescents and adults:

- Self-injury (cutting, burning)
- Inadequate personal hygiene
- Drug and alcohol abuse
- Sexual promiscuity
- Running away from home
- Depression, anxiety
- Suicide attempts
- Fear of intimacy or closeness
- Compulsive eating or dieting

Because of the secretive and private nature of sexual abuse, it's common that you won't see any physical warning signs, such as bleeding or bruising. But if you do, take the person to a doctor or emergency room. Some nurses (sexual assault nurse examiners) are specially trained to support victims emotionally and physically while maintaining any forensic evidence that could be needed in a criminal case. It's also important to get the person tested for sexually transmitted diseases since most can be treated easily.

Looking Out for Perpetrators

We've all heard the expression "a wolf in sheep's clothing," and there's no better way to define a perpetrator. In a previous chapter we covered who perpetrators are and how they operate. Sometimes we have a gut feeling about someone. *Trust your gut.* If you're wrong, you may offend someone. But if you're right—and someone is a perpetrator—if you don't do anything about it, someone *will be* traumatized. In addition, look for these behaviors from adults (teenagers too) when interacting with children:

- Makes others uncomfortable by ignoring social, emotional, or physical boundaries or limits
- Refuses to let a child set any of his or her own limits. Uses teasing or belittling language to keep a child from setting a limit.
- Insists on hugging, touching, kissing, tickling, wrestling with, or holding a child, even when the child does not want this physical contact or attention
- Frequently walks in on children/teens in the bathroom
- Turns to a child for emotional or physical comfort by sharing personal or private information or activities that are normally shared with adults
- Has secret interactions with teens or children (e.g., games, sharing drugs, alcohol, or sexual material) or spends excessive time emailing, text messaging, or calling children/youth
- Insists on or manages to spend uninterrupted time alone with a child

- Seems "too good to be true" (e.g., frequently babysits children for free, takes children on special outings alone, buys children gifts or gives them money for no apparent reason)
- Allows children or teens to consistently get away with inappropriate behaviors
- Frequently points out sexual images or tells dirty or suggestive jokes with children present
- Exposes a child to adult sexual interactions or images without apparent concern
- Is overly interested in the sexuality of a particular child or teen (e.g., talks repeatedly about the child's developing body or interferes with normal teen dating)[6]

None of these things alone, or even combined, can guarantee that a child is being abused or an adult is a child molester. But we need to be on alert, to trust our intuition, to ask for God's discernment, and to *always* act when our red flags are raised.

Responding to Childhood Sexual Abuse

Responding personally and organizationally to childhood sexual abuse is critical. Whether it's responding to the child, to law enforcement, or to some other entity involved, *how* we respond carries great weight with the survivor, their family, our church or organization, and our community. So what should you do when someone comes to you with a report of child sexual abuse?

Believe and report. Believe and report. Believe and report.

It doesn't matter who did it or how it happened. Any time a

minor is sexually abused, *law enforcement must be notified imme-diately.* I cannot emphasize that enough.

I understand there are many perceived barriers to reporting. By reporting the crime, life will never be the same for you (the reporter) and of course for the perpetrator, but keep in mind, the child's life is already forever changed. The child's life has already been significantly altered at this point, and by reporting, you are turning the tables so that justice can be served and other children can be protected. Most law enforcement agencies have units dedicated to crimes against children and also offer services to victims to help guide them through the next steps of the criminal process. Sometimes these services even offer funds for counseling or other medical assis-tance. I was surprised by how many resources were available to me after I reported my abuse to authorities.

How we respond carries great weight with the survivor.

Some fear (or guilt) may come into play when reporting gets another person "in trouble," especially if the sexual abuse occurred within a family. Or a child may be afraid to be taken away from their loved one. Older children may have heard horror stories about what happens in prison and don't want to subject their loved one to that. Breaking up the family is a huge burden that comes with reporting childhood sexual abuse within a family. Since perpetrators are generally known to the child, the child may be afraid of getting a family friend, pastor, or other trusted adult in trouble or causing harm to the abuser's family. Children almost always believe the abuse (and the resulting consequences) is their fault because children have a hard time reconciling the fact that someone they love and trust did something so bad and wrong.

The idea of not being believed is another fear many children have about coming forward, especially when the person who abused them is well-liked or respected in their social circle. A girl I mentored kept her abuse a secret for ten years. Her uncle abused her, and in response to her experience, and without the benefit of good counseling and care, she acted out sexually and used drugs as an outlet to numb herself, gain control, and escape her reality. When she decided to come forward, her family sided with the uncle because he was such a "family man" and the girl was thought to be a trouble maker.

Unfortunately, this happens a lot. In these situations, it's key to reassure the child that any consequence of the abuse rests on the abuser's shoulders—not the survivor's.

I've had to tell myself this *many* times over the years. One of my greatest burdens (and one of the reasons I had such a difficult time coming forward to the Christian organization and to law enforcement) is because I knew Mark's family had to be suffering. His parents, his home church, his wife, his kids, his friends, his coworkers . . . they are all likely grieving too, and that grief is real. This has been one of the most emotionally difficult things to walk through. As Paul says in 1 Corinthians, "If one part [of the body] suffers, every part suffers with it" (1 Corinthians 12:26). I didn't want to be the cause of that suffering. But the truth was, I wasn't. I simply shed light on suffering that had already occurred.

As we said earlier, it's important to believe someone when they share their abuse with you. It takes a great amount of courage for an adult to open up, so imagine how much more courage a child has to muster, not fully grasping the scope of what's happened to them. It is highly unlikely that a child would lie about abuse.

Responding in a Church Setting

In recent years our society has had many scandals involving church leaders, and many of the responses have been dismissive of the victim and supportive of the abuser. This causes significant damage to the victim and other survivors. Interestingly, we've also seen a lot of apologies and backpedaling from the same church leaders when they realize (or have been told by lawyers or law enforcement) that their earlier response of supporting a perpetrator is wildly inappropriate. We cannot and should never excuse the sexual abuse of a child, or defend it, or cover it up in any way.

When you're told about potential abuse, use discernment and discretion with which adults you tell outside of law enforcement. It can be easy to jump into the "prayer/gossip" loop, but your energy should be spent on ensuring that the child is cared for and that the alleged abuser is removed from working with or having access to children until professionals (law enforcement or CPS, *not* pastors or leaders) determine what steps, if any, should be taken.

As supporters, churches, and organizations seeking to support and care for abuse survivors, remember this when an accusation is brought to your attention: *it is not your responsibility to determine whether an allegation is credible.* Research indicates that we are inherently biased toward people in our social circles.[7] It's easier to simply deny that people we know, especially people we perceive to be good or holy, could have committed such evil crimes when faced with the alternative of reporting them. No matter how hard we try, we simply can't be objective, so bringing in a third party such as the authorities to do the investigating—more so, who are trained to do the investigating—is a far better response than investigating ourselves.

Informing Others

If a person is determined to be credibly accused of abuse after you have reported it to law enforcement, it is important to let others know.

After you talk to authorities, you may need to talk to your governing church members, an association leader, a conference, a presbytery, a bishop, a board, or some other supervising entity to determine how to appropriately communicate this to others. After the authorities give you permission to speak to the accused, you may choose to give him or her an opportunity to respond. Until it is determined the accusation is absolutely false (by authorities), the accused should be removed from leadership and/or access to vulnerable people.

The closer the people are to the victim, the sooner those people need to be informed so they can make sure their children haven't been abused. Parents of those with whom the accused has had direct contact, or potential direct contact, should be notified as soon as possible. If abuse has occurred within a church or organization, getting a canned letter or hearing a generic statement from the pastor can be jarring and upsetting, not to mention almost useless when it comes to answering questions that will arise.

If you are a church leader and you want to know how to address this when it comes up in your congregation, ask the authorities or a trauma-informed counselor to help you write a statement. Use their expertise to help you discern how to best communicate with your staff and your congregation, and the public if necessary (which will be more likely than not).

As you are addressing the accusation, you should also provide unconditional care to the survivor, their family, and your congregation. Help them find a supporting person, a counselor, or another church leader who has no conflict of interest. Provide a safe way for other victims to come forward, usually through an independent third-party that has no fiduciary responsibility to your organization. Some families may be intimidated to go to the police, but help them understand that this is incredibly important, and walk with them as they do. If they feel unsafe going to police, together talk to a licensed social worker or counselor so that appropriate steps can be taken.

When you report abuse, you are not ruining someone's good name or gossiping. And you're not violating any biblical commands. Some may argue that the Matthew 18 theology of handling sin mandates that the accusation be dealt with internally, as a matter of church business. But this is flawed. As Christians, we should abide by the law of the land in our country.

Boz Tchividjian, a childhood sexual abuse attorney, advocate, and founder of GRACE (Godly Response to Abuse in the Christian Environment), says: "In this, child sexual abuse is like murder. Anyone who would demand that the family of a murder victim must first follow the Matthew 18 process before calling the police could be criminally charged themselves for being an accessory after the fact. What kind of twisted mind would reason that kidnapping or rape ought to be concealed from the civil authorities while a process of church discipline is pursued first?"[8]

Provide a safe way for other victims to come forward.

In short:

- Believe the child.
- Report to law enforcement.

- Cooperate with law enforcement.
- Intervene if necessary for the safety of the child, and provide crisis care.
- Consult your governing board and a third party to help in providing long-term resources that support the survivor and his or her family.
- Inform the accused about the allegation, and communicate that you have reported it to law enforcement so they can investigate. Remove the accused from contact with children or other vulnerable people if they are not already in jail or prison.
- Seek guidance from trauma-informed professionals for communicating internally with organization members and also with the public.
- Provide a safe, independent means for other victims to come forward.
- Initiate a third-party, professional investigation with an unaffiliated firm such as GRACE to look at the present situation as well as any policies that need to be addressed or reworked.

Moving Forward

All this information can be overwhelming. It's tempting to want a perfect, flawless plan that will prevent abuse and will help you recognize and respond to childhood sexual abuse every time. After all, you don't want a single child to suffer. I wish I could tell you that if you follow all the steps outlined in this book, everything will be okay. I wish it were possible to stop every instance of abuse. No child should have to suffer this way.

Our goal is not perfection; it's to do the best we can with the tools we have, knowing that we *are* doing the right thing and that in doing so we *are* preventing childhood sexual abuse. By learning to recognize abuse when it happens and responding to it in a way that tries to ensure the least amount of pain, we are doing God's work. This is righteous work, and together our collective light will make it more difficult for the darkness to hide.

Conclusion:
A Final Word of Hope

Her angel wings got broken
The moment she crashed down
The fire in her heart disappeared
When she began to drown
Sorting through the memories
Of autumn's late descent
She stumbled around to find
The place her halo went

There she goes . . .
There she goes . . .

She wants to fly again
She wants her tattered wings to mend
She wants to fly again
Take her back
To where it all began

Reflection of heaven
Gone from tarnished eyes
She is hiding
Hiding from you and
Doesn't know why
She can hope for tomorrow
She can't breathe today
Washing away light from stars
With tears she cried yesterday

There she goes . . .
There she goes . . .

—ANNE MARIE MILLER, AGE SEVENTEEN

This is hard work. This is scary work. This is painful work. This is holy work. So many things I wish I could promise you—things I wish were true. As long as there is life on earth, there will also be evil on earth. There will be things that don't make sense. Things that break our hearts. Things that break us. Things that make us sick. Things that disgust us. Things that terrify us. Things that grieve us. There are also things that will encourage us. Things that will revive us.

Psychologist and author Diane Langberg writes, "To take such a complex creature, on who was meant for God and is destroyed by sin, and attempt to understand how the development of that creature can be affected by hideous trauma is to attempt the impossible."[1]

We are attempting the impossible.

During the time I was being abused, I had a student teacher in my English class named Mr. Bennett. He gave us the assignment of keeping a journal during our final year in high school. I rebelled a bit and never wrote a straightforward diary entry of how my day went, which is what he wanted us to do. Instead, I filled it with obscure (and predictably melodramatic) poems and essays.

Somewhere between *Beowulf* and *Lord of the Flies*, he talked about writing and emotion and catharsis. *So that's why I feel this way when I write*, I noticed. I believe this assignment saved my life back then. It was a place for the pain to escape, being pulled out of my body and forever inked onto paper. I could close the cover on it, and put it away . . . if only for a little while.

Mr. Bennett also encouraged us to feel deeply, not to hide away from the uncomfortable feelings, and instead, to allow them to sit with us as friends—awkward friends that you don't really want around but friends nonetheless. Let them shape us and change us. Allow them to become a gift to the world. We are the true philanthropists of society, he said, bestowing the vulnerable essence of existence instead of cash.

For whatever reason, Mr. Bennett's words stuck with me— and do every time I sit down to write something substantial. In 2009, when I wrote *Permission to Speak Freely*, I think I fully recognized how much he had impacted me. *Permission to Speak Freely* was the first time the entire story of my abuse lived on published paper: an open door for anyone to walk through to find that they were not alone. I dedicated that book to him and even tracked him down in Pennsylvania thirteen years after I graduated from high school to thank him face-to-face.

When it was time for me to leave, he walked me to my rental car, our feet crunching on fresh snow. He apologized for not being able to decode what I was writing about all those years ago. He was so new at teaching and so young, still in college and barely old enough to buy beer. I assured him that wasn't his role: to see through my vague poetry, my attempts to sound like E. E. Cummings. He unknowingly and perfectly assumed the role he didn't even know he had: helping me survive one of the most traumatic events in my life by simply being himself and doing what he knew to do—teach.

Most of us are like Mr. Bennett was—green and unfamiliar, unfamiliar with the outlines and particularities, the technicalities, and the generalities of sexual abuse. Perhaps you're a natural nurturer, or maybe you're awkward and anxious around people. It doesn't matter, as long as you are willing.

I want to encourage you to embrace that role, whatever it is. We each play a part in fighting this soul-destroying, life-crushing, endless cycle of malevolence. It's our job to learn and to show up and to be open and, with the very power of Christ that lives and dwells in us, to be. To be available, to be aware, to be approachable. To be bold, to speak up, to cry with, to sit with, to grieve with, to just be. We exist between heaven and earth, caught in the tensions of holy and evil, laughing and weeping, hurting and healing. We will never escape the whiplash of a fallen world until we forever leave this land of the living and cross over to the land of eternal life, where God is making everything new and better.

To quote Dr. Langberg again:

> We are caught in the tensions of holy and evil, laughing and weeping, hurting and healing.

You will stand as a representative of the God who is our refuge, the God who brings hope, the God who hears, the

God who speaks truth, and the God who asks us to choose him. In fact, you will be called on to partake of what was the essence of the Incarnation, bringing God himself down to flesh-and-blood actualities and working his life out through your fingertips. The work of Jesus in this world resulted in redemption. His work in and through you in this world will also result in redemption.[2]

May you be blessed with a holy discomfort and driven by the pursuit of a holy justice as you seek to support those who have experienced the bereavement of abuse. May you be strengthened as you compassionately walk with them toward healing. And may we all be recipients of the grace that is found in healing together.

Appendix A

What Is Trauma?

The Diagnostic and Statistical Manual of Mental Disorders, which is used to diagnose mental health disorders such as post-traumatic stress disorder, or PTSD, defines trauma as occurring when a person is "exposed to: death, threatened death, actual or threatened serious injury, or actual or threatened sexual violence, in the following way(s):*

- Direct exposure
- Witnessing the trauma
- Learning that a relative or close friend was exposed to a trauma
- Indirect exposure to aversive details of the trauma, usually in the course of professional duties (e.g., first responders, medics)."[1]

---

* To save space and for brevity, I have abbreviated the full list of DSM 5 Criteria to the most applicable criteria.

While that definition is a bit technical, we can note a few things from it. Trauma occurs because of an actual experience of violence *or* a threat of violence. And it can happen in several ways. A person can be directly affected by the violence, they can witness it happening to someone else (igniting the mirror neurons we discussed earlier), they can learn about it happening to someone else, and the violence can even affect those who are trying to help a person who has suffered. This last experience is most common among those in the helping professions, such as a nurse, a medic, or a counselor. In chapter 5, I shared some advice on dealing with trauma by proxy, or secondhand trauma, and the need for supporters to be emotionally healthy to help survivors carry the weight of abuse.

The National Institutes of Health widens the definition given above just a bit further, defining it as "a shocking, scary, or dangerous experience that affects someone emotionally."[2] Notice that this means trauma can be both physical and emotional.

How Trauma Affects Us Uniquely

A question I'm frequently asked is: Why do some people respond to small traumas in a way that it takes a lifetime to overcome, but other people appear to be *resilient* in the face of enormous trauma? A variety of factors play into this response, but the simplest answer is that everybody, and *every body* (note the difference) experiences, reacts to, and stores events in their bodies differently. Here are a few reasons why some people are more resilient in the face of life's challenges than others.

Epigenetics: This is a fancy word to describe the variety of things that can be passed on to us beyond our DNA. Epigenetics includes what happens to us as we develop in the womb and how your mother and father's life experiences may affect the makeup of your brain and body chemicals, your hormones, and your cell biology. These characteristics are inherently passed on to you, influencing your overall personality.

Early childhood experiences: The experiences we have as children profoundly shape who we are and how we grow and develop. How your parents or caregivers interacted with you as a child can affect the way you respond to other interpersonal experiences, including trauma. This is true even when we don't remember these experiences.

Prior trauma: Those who have experienced prior trauma are more likely to experience difficulties coping with additional trauma. In the most complex cases, the negative effects are a form of PTSD called complex post-traumatic stress disorder. The more that these traumas pile up, the heavier the burden is to carry, and the more difficult it is to unwind all the threads of the various trauma.

The three items noted above are largely out of our control. We can't change who we are or the circumstances of our formation and birth. And we don't have control over childhood experiences or traumatic events that happened to us. But two things are within our control, and these have been scientifically proven to increase resiliency, or the ability to withstand traumatic events without suffering much beyond the actual experience. These factors are:

Mastery: A term used by psychologists to describe an "external locus of control"—the ability to influence and control one's circumstances and outcomes. The opposite of this trait (having an "internal locus of control") describes what happens when people think they have no control over their circumstances in life. In other words, they feel powerless. Mastery either says, "I can get through this" (external locus) or "Why does everything always happen to me?" (internal locus). To a degree, we are all asking a mix of both questions. The good news is that you have some measure of control over this factor. You can retrain your brain and improve your mastery over your circumstances and outcomes.

If you are a Christian, you know that ultimately God is in control and sovereign, but you understand that he gives you the gifts of free will and the ability to choose your actions. This means you can pursue resilience. Some see this as the perseverance or faithfulness referred to in the Bible (Philippians 3:13–15; Romans 12:21; James 1:12). Job also showed resilience during his trials. In many ways, our belief in God's sovereignty can enable and empower our resiliency in the face of adversity.

Social support: This last factor can be a tough one for people who experience trauma or who grew up in an unstable household. When we experience trauma, we often experience shame and distrust and have a tendency to isolate ourselves, thinking we are safer alone. But social support is essential to a trauma survivor's recovery. It takes intentionality and commitment for this to happen, by both supporters and survivors.

Sometimes it's difficult for supporters to reach out to a loved one who is hurting, because they don't know what to say or don't want to be intrusive. And often it's difficult for survivors to reach out for help amid their fear and shame.

The truth is that every one of us is wired uniquely, with a combination of all the above factors influencing us to various degrees and with various experiences. No two people experience trauma in the same way. Some people are genetically predisposed to more easily recover, while others will hopelessly fight with all their might and never fully recover physically, mentally, relationally, and spiritually. Empathy is necessary in every case. Some of us will never fully know the depth of hardship that happens when someone is abused.

But even if we cannot fully empathize, we can seek to better understand. In the next section, we'll consider some of the common problems survivors face. I've broken them down into separate areas of health, but note that our bodies are designed holistically, so you can never truly separate these from one another. Each area influences the others.

BODY

The physical symptoms of trauma will be unique to each person, depending on a variety of factors that we've already discussed. Trauma causes a change in stress hormones such as cortisol and adrenaline and also in the way our nervous system communicates with our brain, heart, muscles, temperature, and other organ functions. These changes can be acute and last for only a short period of time, allowing the body to recover once the threat has passed, or if someone is more vulnerable to the effects of trauma, the changes can become chronic, often lasting years or even the rest of someone's life.

OBESITY AND CHRONIC ILLNESS

Millions of people struggle with chronic diseases such as diabetes, high blood pressure, or cholesterol. While these diseases are typical for people in developed countries with access to processed and fast food, many times the underlying causes for indulging in that diet is because of a search for emotional—not physical—satiation.

Studies show that childhood sexual abuse victims are more likely to be overweight or obese as adults, having as much as 20 percent more of a risk for females than compared with those not abused. Scientists think this happens for a couple of reasons: neurobiological (a brain/body response that can be consciously changed) as well as survival (an unconscious response).[3]

On a neurobiological basis, the trauma of abuse affects levels of dopamine and norepinephrine, the reward and "feel-good" chemicals that get released in your brain. Those who suffer abuse are left with a decreased ability to feel pleasure. This is where substance abuse—including abusing food—begins. Survivors often abuse alcohol, food, or recreational drugs to escape or achieve a higher level of those chemicals that they are lacking, and the abuse turns into addiction.

On the other hand, the body's limbic system, which controls our instinctual survival, can interpret the trauma as life threatening.[4] If the body doesn't recover, the brain doesn't know that it's safe. In the days of hunting and gathering, when food could be scarce, this instinct kept humans alive. But a survivor's body doesn't know there's a Kroger down the road or a McDonald's on the way to pick up your kid from school. It just hears one message: survival equals eating. Erik Hemmingsson, an associate professor of medicine at Karolinska University in Sweden, said, "If you think of the body as a clever organism, if it's exposed to something that's threatening, it protects itself by making sure there are plenty of calories on board."[5] This, combined with elevated stress hormones, means extra fat can be stored away, even in people who don't overeat.

The American College of Obstetricians and Gynecologists (ACOG) reported these common physical ailments in a recent study: "Chronic and diffuse pain, especially abdominal or pelvic pain, lower pain threshold, anxiety and depression, self-neglect, and eating disorders have been attributed to childhood sexual abuse. Adults abused as children are four to five times more likely to have abused alcohol and illicit drugs. They are also twice as likely to smoke, be physically inactive, and be severely obese."[6]

REPRODUCTIVE AND SEXUAL ISSUES

Since I was sixteen—the same time as my abuse— reproductive system issues and pelvic pain have plagued me, the latter being a common experience of sexual abuse victims. I also developed endometriosis, something no one in my family had ever suffered before. I continually had painful ovarian cysts, inconsistent cycles with missed periods or menorrhagia (profuse and heavy menstrual bleeding), and tremendous amounts of physical pain. I had several laparoscopic procedures and have been on various hormone therapies my entire life (I still am to this day). After suffering two miscarriages, my husband and I conceived in a biologically miraculous way, and by a scientific miracle of God's grace, I had a healthy pregnancy.

My doctors thought that my hormones would even out after I gave birth. Unfortunately, my issues continued, and when our daughter was eight months old, I had to have a radical hysterectomy, where my uterus, remaining fallopian tube (I had an ectopic pregnancy and lost my left tube previously), ovaries, and cervix were removed. As I walked out of the hospital the day after my procedure, the nurses noted that I "looked like a new woman," and my family noticed a remarkable change in my appearance—my skin was bright, my eyes were clear, and even my posture was better. Though the abuse likely cost me many body parts, I was happy to finally feel different. Pelvic pain had been my norm for twenty years, and my body was finally at peace.

The same study from the ACOG finds that "disturbances of desire, arousal, and orgasm may result from the association between sexual activity, violation, and pain. Gynecologic problems, including chronic pelvic pain, dyspareunia, vaginismus, and nonspecific vaginitis, are common diagnoses among survivors."[7]

Male sexual abuse survivors face reproductive problems too, including things such as erectile dysfunction, painful intercourse, and pelvic pain.

All that to say, the trauma from sexual abuse stays with your body *years* after the actual instances of abuse have passed.

INSOMNIA

Insomnia has also been an issue since my late teens. I've undergone sleep studies that revealed that even when I am asleep, I rarely enter the restorative sleep cycles we all need to be rested. My brain "woke up" over two hundred times in eight hours, which indicated it was always on alert, hypervigilant for threats. I was eventually referred to a sleep neurologist for more studies, but after reviewing my history and records, the neurologist simply stated, "Your insomnia is directly related to your PTSD and abuse. To resolve it, you've got to continue healing from your trauma."

In unhealthier days, I would medicate myself to sleep using a bottle (sometimes two) of wine and antianxiety medication. But even then I didn't sleep—I just blacked out under the appearance of sleep. Now that I don't drink alcohol, I am on an intense sleep routine that includes good sleep hygiene, going to bed consistently early (usually by 9 p.m.), waking up early (usually by 6 a.m.—I find if I sleep longer, I feel horrible), and a specific medication regimen that uses various prescriptions, herbs, oils, and over-the-counter treatment. If the average person took the medication I take to sleep each night, they would probably face respiratory distress. But the adrenaline in my body is so high that it causes my metabolism to run high, and the measures I take to sleep are barely enough to knock me out into the right brain waves for true rest. Sadly, my story is far too common among survivors.

Other Physical Effects

What's interesting is after the Christian organization interviewed me, a lot of trauma presented as physical symptoms. I developed an arrhythmia which required two cardiac ablations. I had to have my gallbladder and appendix removed. I had severe acid reflux. But once I went through a season of healing my trauma through therapy, my body has mostly realigned, and I don't have many chronic physical health symptoms outside the insomnia and hormone replacement therapy. Again, all that to say, the trauma of sexual abuse stays with you—even your sleep patterns—for years, even a *lifetime* for some people.

MIND

The mind is perhaps the most affected by sexual abuse, but it is a part of the survivor's body that goes unseen. We can't read minds, and humans are great at masking what's going on internally. Abuse can affect everything from our emotions and mood to our attention and intellectual capacity.

EMOTIONS AND MENTAL HEALTH

Understandably, experiencing a trauma can provoke a diverse range of emotions, both immediately after the trauma and long after it has taken place. Here we will talk about the common experiences and damage to a person's mental health that generally come with sexual abuse. Not everyone who is abused experiences these symptoms, nor are the symptoms themselves indicative of abuse (other circumstances, genetics, and temperament can cause depression, for example). These symptoms are experienced on a spectrum from mild to severe, and seasons can come and go.

- *Disassociation:* This often happens during instances of abuse as a protection mechanism. But it can manifest consciously or subconsciously in other areas of emotional health. Disassociation brings about feelings of numbness, denial, disorientation, separation from body or reality, or amnesia around the event and other childhood memories.

- *General stress and anxiety:* These cause phobias, anxiety attacks, or panic attacks. There are several anxiety disorders: *general anxiety*, which is the state of always being anxious; *social anxiety*, or the fear of social situations; and *panic disorder*, which is when severe anxiety manifests in waves, often causing a panic attack. *Panic attacks* are periods of extreme fear, often coupled with physical symptoms such as severe chest pain or a sense that one cannot breathe. Panic can cause a person to think he or she is legitimately dying.
- *Flashbacks:* This is a mental rerun or reexperiencing of one's abuse, and the anxiety that comes along with it can be debilitating. We can't always know what will trigger us until we are already submerged in an experience. For me, some of my flashbacks happen when I see a midnineties Pontiac Grand Am, when I pass the apartments or park where my abuse happened, or when I look at certain actors who have eyes similar to Mark's. Some flashbacks happen in dreams (or more appropriately, nightmares). Survivors can also be triggered by other senses, such as scent. For example, certain colognes can easily bring back a survivor's memories of how their abuser smelled.
- There are also physical forms of "flashbacks." Being touched in a specific way, whether we cognitively remember it or our body simply recalls it without our overt knowledge, can cause survivors to experience anxiety. This can be confusing, frustrating, and scary when it happens within a consensual, adult relationship. Many times survivors don't know why they are recoiling from appropriate and loving touch from a family member or spouse, but they recoil

all the same. Their body is undergoing a "flashback" and responding defensively to it.

- *Guilt, shame, and blame:* Those who have been abused often think they are somehow responsible for their abuse. They didn't say no (usually because they were practicing the *fawn* response to abuse to keep themselves safe), they were dressed in something other than a sweat suit, or out of fear they didn't tell someone immediately. This negative thinking circulates in the survivor's mind like a hurricane that never moves away after coming ashore. New pathways physically develop in our minds, like running water creating crevices in sand, solidifying these thoughts. Survivors think we're worthless, and that the whole thing is our own fault.

- *Depression:* This is the most widely reported response to abuse. Depression in survivors is partially linked to constant negative thoughts and inability to control anxiety. Symptoms of depression are feeling "down" for more than a couple of weeks, inconsistent sleep (which then contributes more to the depression because of disturbed hormones), poor eating habits, and sometimes suicidal thoughts.

- *Suicidal thinking:* Abuse leaves the survivor hopeless and exhausted. It takes immense amounts of strength to function, and there are times when many survivors want to escape from reality, and tragically, they think their only relief from suffering is death. Suicidal thoughts are more common in abuse survivors than you might think, and the stigma surrounding these thoughts keeps survivors isolated and afraid to talk.

HYPERVIGILANCE

Hypervigilance is when our bodies are on high alert for potential threats. After trauma, some survivors see *everything* as a threat. Sometimes we don't have any control of these intrusive thoughts. Survivors are easily startled. I can hear my husband come home from work when the garage door opens and he steps into our mudroom, but if I don't *see* him come into the kitchen to give me a hug, I jump and my heart pounds. This happens when he is trying to show me *affection*, and yet my body responds as if I'm experiencing trauma.

Another way survivors express hypervigilance is black-and-white thinking. It's easy to go from peacefully sitting at home, snuggled up with my dog on the couch, sipping tea, and working on this book to sitting on the bathroom floor terrified. That recently happened to me. Let me explain.

Right before this book was due to my publisher, I booked a couple of nights away at an Airbnb home in Dallas. I woke up after a great night's sleep, made some tea, and got to work. I started writing about the mental health effects of trauma when I heard a helicopter and some sirens.

The house was a couple of miles from the hospital I work at, which has a helipad. I thought—logically—that the helicopter was probably just on its way to the hospital. The sirens could mean anything.

"But," my mind started wondering . . . "What if?"

What if the helicopter is a police helicopter and they're trying to find some dangerous fugitive? This house backs up to the woods and a creek. It would be the perfect hiding place for someone on the run from the police. I didn't lock my car. What if he is hiding out in my car? Maybe Pinky (my dog) and I should leave until it's safe. But what if the fugitive is in my car? We'll get held hostage. And the door on this place is pretty old—I bet he could kick it in.

To put my mind at ease, I logged on to a website that lists all the open police calls in Dallas. Right at the top was one for armed robbery and a shooting. I wasn't familiar with the street name, so I looked it up. It was right across the main street from where I was staying! My suspicions were right!

Do I stay? Do I leave? What do I do? I locked the door, put a chair in front of it, and lowered all the blinds. I called the police nonemergency line and let them know my proximity to the crime and that the helicopter was still circling.

Am I safe?

The dispatcher asked whether police were on my street.

Well, no.

She then asked whether I saw anything suspicious.

Well, no.

"You're fine," she reassured me. "Just maybe stay in the house until you don't hear the helicopters. But unless the police tell you otherwise, don't worry about it."

Even though the police themselves confirmed that I was in no perceivable danger, I stayed in the bathroom, on the floor, out of sight until the helicopter went away about twenty minutes later.

That is hypervigilance.

When planes fly over our house, it's only a matter of time before one crashes through the front door or drops a wing on our roof, causing the house (and us) to be incinerated.

When our daughter coughs in the middle of the night, I worry she's in respiratory distress.

Every spider is poisonous, probably a mutated hybrid black widow *and* brown recluse.

The gas stove surely has a leak and the carbon monoxide detectors broke without us knowing.

I say I love you almost superstitiously, just in case it's the last time I see a family member, and I've had a will since I was nineteen, just in case.

The funny thing is that I've been in therapy for most of my adult life (working on having healthier behaviors), I'm on a good medication regimen, I'm fully aware of my tendency to believe the worst, and yet the most innocuous, mundane things still make my brain spin all the time.

If you met me on the street and we went to have coffee, or even if we saw each other regularly, without knowing my story, you wouldn't be able to tell just how intense this anxiety is and how much joy it steals from my everyday life. You wouldn't notice how I keep glancing at the exits and making sure nobody is carrying a gun or how I would dive under what table to protect myself in case of a shooting. You may see me take my anxiety medicine, but I'd be sneaky about it. You wouldn't know how desperately I want these issues to go away.

I polled some people regarding their experiences with trauma and their struggles with the subsequent hypervigilance that followed their abuse. Here are some of the common themes and responses that came back:

- "Double/triple checking to make sure I unplug hot appliances (straightener, iron, etc.)."
- "Checking multiple times to make sure doors are locked."
- "If a family member is running late, I've been known to compulsively check their location on Find My iPhone because I'm sure they've been in an accident."

- "Obsessing that my children will be kidnapped because they won't know what to do."
- "I am pretty certain I am going to die because a train's weight is going to collapse a bridge as I pass under it, so I speed up."
- "I held my kid's hand in parking lots until they were preteens because I was sure they'd get run over."
- "I have an exaggerated startle reflex when surprised. I literally jump and gasp for air."
- "I tremble at sudden loud noises and imagine disaster in *every* situation."

ATTENTION AND FOCUS

Abuse can cause survivors to be easily distracted. Many children who are abused often get diagnosed with attention deficit disorder (ADD), which can continue into adulthood. The inability to focus on tasks or simply get through daily functioning is largely due to hypervigilance—or always being on guard.

PERSPECTIVE AND POINT OF VIEW

A survivor's emotional and mental perspective can be clouded. When someone has been violated in such an intimate way, it's incredibly difficult to trust again. And depending on who violated that trust, the perspective of a survivor toward a person like their abuser can be irrationally dark. I have a difficult time trusting church leaders and pastors, especially those who work with children. Our daughter goes to a preschool at a local church that has had perfect marks from the state department, and all employees are thoroughly background checked. The school even has limited access to the classrooms through a key fob system only the director and assistant director possess, and they have cameras at the entryways and in every room.

Despite all this, my anxiety is high when I think about what could happen. There are no cameras in the bathrooms (that serve as public restrooms on weekends when church happens), so what if something happened in a bathroom? What about the other parents or contractors? It would be tough—but not impossible— for something to happen to our daughter. And what about once when she's in grade school, or middle school, or high school, or college?

After abuse, a veil of darkness and evil color everything. Though we've been freely given joy through Christ, abuse steals that away from us, and it's hard to get it back. Most of the time, our hearts are too weary to fight for it.

HEART

Relationships are undoubtedly tough after abuse. Most abuse takes place within established relationships, so trust takes on a whole new meaning. Trust in new relationships becomes difficult, strained, confusing, and grievous. But it can also (potentially) be an opportunity for redemption.

The identity and relationship of the abuser to the victim directly influences those types of relationships in the victim's future. For example, if an abuser was a coach, victims will have a hard time engaging coaches from then on. My abuse came from someone I thought romantically loved me, and someone I believed I loved. Thus, my romantic relationships have never been easy—I either refused to get emotionally (or physically) intimate with some, or in order to feel powerful (especially immediately after my abuse), I jumped into quick, physical-only relationships with guys

I barely knew, where *I* was in control, or so I thought. Having the upper hand sexually made me assume I could be the one in charge of what happened and that I wouldn't have to be helpless ever again. Once I came to realize, through therapy, that this is a normal yet destructive response for abusive victims, I stopped and learned healthier habits. Many abuse victims often act out in a sexually compulsive manner in an attempt to regain the power that was taken from them. Statistics show that "survivors are more likely to have had 50 or more intercourse partners, have had a sexually transmitted infection, and engage in risk-taking behaviors that place them at risk of contracting human immunodeficiency virus (HIV)."[8]

Because the church historically has not responded to abuse well, or how victims reel from it or try to regain their voice and agency in the world, pastors and leaders often assume that the victim is simply promiscuous. *See, look, she's sexually deviant anyway. That wasn't abuse. Her current life only proves that she seduces men.* Or my personal favorite: *She has a Jezebel spirit.* They don't understand that the victim may be self-medicating and desperately trying to restore what was taken from her—she's just going about it in the wrong way.

For years I never shared the details about the sexual component of my abuse. The first time anyone heard details was when the Christian organization investigated it. I told only a small handful of people because I was too afraid of being judged. It's just easier to keep my heart on lockdown.

In my marriage, I go through seasons of having a healthy sexual desire to having no sexual desire, and that's not my husband's fault at all. Since coming forward a year ago, it's been increasingly

---

* As we said in the eighties, "Gag me with a spoon!"

difficult to block out the trauma of my abuse and to be intimate with my husband. I feel dirty, used, broken, and unworthy. Tim does everything he can to combat my feelings, and he is incredibly patient. It can be a strain on us, though, and I know it's a strain on other marriages and relationships as well.*

When abuse happens in a family, the dynamics can explode. If the abuse is incestuous, the innocent parent can refuse to believe his or her spouse is capable of abuse, leaving the child ultimately betrayed by both parents. One of the main reasons children don't report abuse within family systems is they're afraid to break their family up, and they're confused about what healthy love is. This carries over into adult relationships too. Survivors may be "less skilled at self-protection. They are more apt to accept being victimized by others,"[9] and "this tendency to be victimized repeatedly may be the result of general vulnerability in dangerous situations and exploitation by untrustworthy people."[10]

SPIRIT

A person's spirituality, and view of God if they are a believer, is dramatically affected by sexual abuse. So many theological questions arise when we're harmed.

- Why did God let this happen?
- Why didn't he protect me?
- Why don't people believe me?
- Where is God's justice in all this?

---

* If you're a survivor, highlight this sentence. You are not alone. Now share it with your spouse or significant other: You also are not alone. Thank you for your patience with us.

- Why won't my abuser confess what happened? Is God not working in his soul to feel conviction over what he did?

I wish I had a blanket answer for all these questions—a cure-all for you—but I don't. These are still questions I wrestle with daily. If God knew I was already experiencing a faith crisis, lonely, and looking for help and friends in order to serve him, why did this man (who had the appearance of godliness) groom me and abuse me? Why did the Christian organization not really hold him accountable after they determined he "more likely than not" abused me? Why do I still, almost daily, have to clarify for pastors—shepherds of the faith—that sexual abuse is both a criminal act and a moral failing? Why do I have to keep saying, as if it's unclear, that part of being a good citizen and honoring our governing authorities is reporting abuse when it happens, as we are required to do by law? Forgiveness is important, yes. But so is criminal justice and legal action when necessary. Those trusted to care and spiritually direct their flocks don't always subscribe to that idea, and to see them push back when other leaders try to do the right thing—stand up and reconcile with victims—well, it's another painful strike against my faith. Worse than that, it doesn't tell the truth about God—the One who loves, draws near to, and vindicates the vulnerable.

I have grown up in the church. I have some seminary education. I don't expect life to be easy, and I know some of the most faithful servants of God suffered the most in life. So I don't have an unrealistic hope for an easy life. I don't buy into the prosperity gospel of health and wealth for all, if we just believe a little more. I wish I could just believe God is *with* me. I cognitively know that, but I relationally don't feel as though that is my experience. This is fairly common for survivors. I talked in chapter 2 about what supporters can do to encourage (and not hurt) those trying to recover spiritually from abuse, but cherry-picking verses, comparing traumas, and even prayer can have the opposite effect on us, increasing our anger at God. Sharing that we're angry with God isn't easy to do in faith environments either, so we often internalize it all, which can leave us bitter, cynical, and cut off relationally and spiritually. It's easy for us to think, "If I tell them about my abuse, they're going to give me the 'pity face' and say they're sorry and then tell me how God is going to work it for my good or how he has plans for me or how he will never give us things we can't handle." We just want to be heard . . . we're not a project that needs fixing.

Conclusion

Overall, I hope this appendix helped you understand a little more about trauma. I hope you can see the ways trauma has affected a survivor in more ways than just the abusive incident(s) itself, and how mental, physical, emotional, and spiritual ramifications follow them everywhere they go. I hope, more than anything, that this appendix helps you overflow in compassion for survivors and ignites a desire in you to walk alongside them toward healing.

Appendix B

Understanding
Traumatic Memory

$\mathcal{S}$ome of the common questions I receive regarding traumatic
memories are:

- Do survivors ever embellish their stories?
- Why can't people remember the details of these
  significant events?
- Where do suppressed memories go?
- How can someone have an emotional or physical
  response (anxiety, depression, PTSD, decreased
  sexual arousal) to their trauma when they can't even
  remember it?
- Can childhood memories or forgotten memories be
  trusted?

Forgotten Memories

Most people don't report abuse because of fear and shame. Someone rarely forgets what happened, at least in a broad sense. Someone can generally recall, without specific detail, that they were abused. I know I was sexually abused. While my body and mind disassociated (also called dissociative amnesia) for my perceived survival, there was never a moment after my abuse when I didn't know that I was abused.

So as I talk about forgotten memories, it is in reference to people recalling both *details* of abuse and *the event* of abuse. The process of recollection is the same, but I thought it was important to note that just because someone doesn't recall specific details of his or her abuse, it does not invalidate the experience.

Implanted or False Memories

In the 1980s and 1990s, there was a lot of controversy around "repressed" or "suppressed" memories, or memories that aren't consciously recalled, especially when dealing with traumatic experiences. This happened because books written by unethical psychologists proclaimed a "miracle approach" to helping people recover memories of incest and childhood abuse.

Celebrity therapists got on board first, which opened the doors for the general population. After a client would disclose some mental health problem, such as depression or anxiety, the therapist would tell them it was a result of sexual abuse in their childhood. The person wouldn't recall their abuse, but the therapist would persist, strongly correlating their mood disorder to abuse that happened. Once the client accepted the possibility that they could have been abused, the psychologist would embed false memories of abuse by asking specific—and leading—questions by having their clients describe what it looked like. Asking "Can you elaborate on how your father molested you? Were you in your bed?" allowed the client, already vulnerable and trusting of their therapist, to create a new narrative justifying whatever mental illness from which they suffered.

It turned into a nightmare. People heard how their friend learned they were abused and repressed their memory, so maybe their depression or anxiety was linked to forgotten childhood sexual abuse as well, and they'd seek help from the same therapist. Many people were falsely accused of abuse, and some were even arrested and tried. The media rode out the sensational wave, furthering damage to people's reputations and credibility. One of the most heartbreaking things about this (outside of those who suffered the consequences of false accusations) was that the people alleging abuse truly believed they had been abused because of how the therapists implanted memories. They weren't maliciously accusing anybody—they genuinely believed they had been abused. In reality, their abuse was committed by their therapists, who used them for financial gain and prestige.

Psychologist Elizabeth Loftus was one of the first people to suspect that this wasn't legitimate science, and she set out to show that memories could be implanted into vulnerable people. She says, "While I couldn't prove that a particular memory emerging from therapy was false, perhaps I could step around to the other side of the problem. Through careful experimental design and controlled studies, perhaps I could provide a theoretical framework for the creation of false memories, showing that it is possible to create an entire memory for a traumatic event that never happened."[1]

She used the same methods as these other "therapists" and designed an experiment that proved this ideology false, unreliable, and unethical. Those therapists fought back, trying to hang on to their profitable practices, and Loftus continued conducting experiments, each one with a wilder or crazier allegation that obviously had to be fabricated.

One of her final and most absurd experiments using these bogus methods convinced thirty people that they had been licked (and sometimes seduced) by the Disney character Pluto during a childhood trip to Disneyland.[2] When asked leading questions and told strategically suggested events in a safe setting by a trustworthy person, people can be steered to believe just about anything.

Loftus's point was made. Because of the amount of damage that had unraveled, the practices by these therapists ended. Many of the earlier "victims" recanted their stories and retracted allegations.

The stigma behind this unethical therapy is what causes so many people today to be wary of memories that return to a victim. We remember significant days in our lives. Wouldn't a traumatic experience such as abuse be one of these easily recalled events?

As someone who grew up in the nineties, I vaguely remember the false memory scandal in the news, and I think it affected my general belief on the topic. After all, I confidently remembered a lot of what happened in my own abuse experience. I remembered where and when Mark and I met, where his apartment was and the layout of it, how he dressed, comments he made to me, and even what I wore on certain occasions. I remember his AOL screen name, the car he drove, and where we went the few times we ventured out in public. I remember what kind of ice cream we bought and the store.

But the science of memory is not as black-and-white as people may think, and with advancing technology in brain imaging, we are learning even more about how the brain receives, processes, stores, and retrieves memories. Let's take a look at the basic physiology.

Creating Memories and Other Basic Memory Physiology

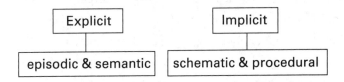

The two main categories of memory are implicit (unconscious) and explicit (conscious).

Explicit, conscious memory can be more specifically defined as episodic and semantic.

- Episodic memory relates to remembering events and the details associated with them (for example, perhaps you went to Austin, Texas, with your boyfriend in 1987, and you had the best BBQ ever at Rudy's. On the way home it was raining, and you hydroplaned off the road).
- Semantic memory is more fact based, such as knowing that Austin is the capital of Texas and that a red light means stop.[3]

Similarly, implicit, unconscious memory can be broken down into schematic and procedural memory.

- Schematic memory allows you the ability to create expectations (If you walk into a restaurant, you'll see tables, booths, patrons, and you'll eat food—perhaps that fresh spring roll you had last time—it was super good!).
- Procedural memory is what guides us as we tie our shoes, use gross motor function (such as walking or running), or complete everyday tasks without thinking much about it, such as cooking or cleaning.[4]

These memories live in different parts of our brain, which is why when people have a brain injury or develop dementia, they may lose their ability to recall (almost always) explicit memories, but their implicit memory stays intact: they remember how to tie their shoes and how to write down words or do puzzles (although in some cases, even this part of the brain is affected too, which causes these kinds of skills to degenerate).

When we have an experience, our nervous system receives it using our senses. Our brain responds and tells our body (both conscious and unconscious) what to do. The brain stores all the input and reactions in neurons in various parts of the brain, depending on the sense used or action resulted.

Hard Drives and Partitions: Storing and Recalling

Have you ever had to defragment your hard drive or run programs that help you see where your information is getting stored on your computer? Though the human body is not a machine, a hard drive is a great analogy to consider when talking about our brains and about memory. We can use the idea that our brain, for the most part, is our hard drive. Our memories are stored there.

When our memories are experienced, transmitted, and stored, they are deposited in all different parts of our brain—not just one big block or hard drive. Distinct parts of our brain—such as the hippocampus and the amygdala, for example—are partitions of our brain's hard drive, each storing different information. Let's look at a simple example of how our brain stores and recalls memory: I'll use my daughter, who's three.

When Charlotte was about seventeen months old, she was interested in potty training (don't call us lucky; it took her another year to meet this milestone). She would climb up on the potty and situate herself on it but would never actually go. At one point, she kind of fell into the water in the bowl—a traumatic experience for a toddler who doesn't quite understand the details of going potty or the function of the water. In her mind, I imagine she experienced a lot of sensory input:

Sight: She was in the bathroom on a tall (to her) toilet.

Touch: She felt herself falling and the cold water on her skin.

Smell: Nothing remarkable (thank goodness).

Sound: The splashing of the water, me probably rushing to her aid and saying, "Oh no!"

Taste: Nothing remarkable (let's hope).

Each one of those senses are stored in different parts of the brain. We have the things she saw transmitting into her visual cortex in the occipital lobe (partition #1). The sense of touch and movement go to her hippocampus, where spatial memory is stored (partition #2). Her memory of the sounds (my voice, the water) are all being sent over and stored in the auditory cortex found in the temporal lobe (partition #3). As for emotions involved, my reaction of urgency and her experience of fear are sent to the amygdala (partition #4).

For Charlotte to recall this memory, her brain (the main hard drive) has to send a signal out to the partitions and say, "Hey, brothers and sisters of gray matter, unite! It's time to recall a memory!" Those partitions then send their respective bits of encoded information and data to the hard drive, which reassembles these bits into a cohesive memory. Amazing!

One of the struggles we had for a long time as Charlotte potty trained is that she would not sit on a "big" potty. Even if her clothes were on and the lid was closed, she backed into a corner and said, "I don't want to. I'm scared." She'd go on her tiny portable potty without any problem. But because this memory was so encoded in her (without many other negative memories competing for space), it was a big deal to her. (Dear Future Charlotte, I hope this anecdote doesn't embarrass you too much when you're older. You're such a big girl. And I'm glad we're no longer spending your college fund money on Hello Kitty diapers. Love, Mom.)

Mixed Signals in Memory Recall

If you've ever had something "on the tip of your tongue," it's most likely because that little piece of data—which you're sure you know, and you probably do—is stuck in the system somewhere. Darn you, sluggish neurons!

As I've said before but in case you've forgotten,* with trauma, our brain and body have one primary response: survive. The data taken in is stored in the brain in whatever way that will keep our body the safest. The bits of information do not always go to places they are supposed to, or places that are easily accessible later. And we don't have control over how our brain decides to store things when it comes to trauma such as abuse experiences.

I heard a great way to describe the feeling of having anxiety or panic: recall the emotional and physical sensation you get when you trip going up or down the stairs. For a split second, you have a rush of adrenaline, and you're acutely hyperfocused. Most people feel a physical sensation in their chest as their heart rate accelerates, and without thinking, you brace yourself in the best way to keep your balance or catch yourself if you do fall. That is your brain keeping your body safe, with no conscious thought by you.

Your brain cannot decipher what is an *actual* threat versus a *perceived* threat versus a *remembered* threat. It only knows there is a threat, whether it is consciously or subconsciously present. After someone experiences any trauma, the brain thinks: *I must keep the rest of me safe.*

The Locked Box

Significantly traumatic memories are stored and locked away in a *completely separate* compartment of memory, away from the

---

* Forgotten? . . . Get it? A memory joke? Sorry. I had to.

recollection of our day-to-day expressions of explicit and implicit memories. Once our mind and body determine we are no longer at risk (emotionally or physically), we have a shot at uncovering some of those stored memories, *but not until then*—not until our brain decides it is safe. This is usually a subconscious process. And in many cases, traumatic memories don't always come back, but it is possible for some of them to surface. To restate: that's possible only once our brain decides that the threat has passed.

These memories can change the physical properties of our brain's topography when they're placed out of reach from other nontraumatic memories. This is why traumatic events such as abuse can be forgotten and then recalled with great and accurate detail years later, especially when they are emotionally triggered. They are instinctual and incredibly exact.

In the recent book *Memory*, Megan Giroux contributed to a chapter entitled "Reconstructing the Past." There she said, "During the consolidation phase of memory formation, the amygdala modulates hippocampal memories through the actions of stress hormones. The net result is that events that elicit strong emotional responses, and are likely to be more important for survival, are also more likely to be well and more accurately remembered at a later time. These types of memories are thus less susceptible to distortion and, in some cases, impossible to forget."[5] I realize it sounds a little paradoxical that forgotten memories are—at the same time—impossible to forget. This is the complexity that is traumatic memory.

Memories created by children versus memories created by adults are functionally the same, but time, experience, and other memories can affect the way we recall things. When something traumatic happens to a child and it is recalled later in life, it is statistically more accurate than an adult recalling a traumatic experience that was recent. But data continually shows us that traumatic memories in general are highly accurate, *especially when the traumatic experience happened to someone when they were young.* [6]

If a survivor wants to, or needs to, recall something, it usually requires slow, trauma-informed therapy that allows the body to feel safe again, which then tells the mind that it's okay to let these memories out. There is a high ethical bar for trauma therapists. They're only able to guide a survivor to express how they *feel* about what they are remembering, never inserting details or suggestions that the survivor doesn't remember.

The Fear in Remembering

Here I must stop to say something important: *If you are not trained to counsel trauma survivors, do not counsel trauma survivors.* You will create another trauma in the process. Do not unlock the safe-deposit box. Don't even ask for the key. You can help survivors work through the things they know, but do not ask additional questions. If a survivor says she has been abused, don't ask her to describe it (unless you are, in fact, a trauma-informed* therapist. In that case, I should probably be reading your book, not the other way around!). Offer to listen, and let them know you are a safe person. It may even be helpful to let them know ahead of time that you are not going to ask details about what happened. Though going deeper in friendship is typically a good thing, the trend of "going there" with someone, and hitting a new level of

---

* Which simply means understanding the way trauma can affect a person and interacting with that person accordingly.

depth and trust and honesty in the relationship should not be applied to a survivor who is sharing about memories of abuse. Do not force a survivor to "go there"—*they will not be helped by this.*

Over the last few years, especially when being asked specific questions about my abuse, or encountering something related to my abuse (for instance, finding the receipt for the picture frame I bought Mark in an old purse at my parents' house years later, or seeing the rerun of the Oprah episode, or discovering an old journal with Mark's name on it), I'll remember something new that reminds me that I don't remember everything and there may be more. Sometimes it solidifies something I already know, but more often than not, it raises more questions—and more fear—about my abuse and what I'm not remembering.

This has been one of the more difficult sections to write. The organization where Mark worked sent me the entire transcript of my interview with them, and I read over it so I could see through new, more-trained eyes, how I remembered things and how they asked the questions. I found myself feeling a roller coaster of emotions: anger, terror, sadness, shame. I was angry at their approach to interviewing me—what seemed to be a search to catch me off guard or an effort to reconcile the gaps in my memory.

Their method, though most likely unbeknownst to them and unbeknownst to *far* too many organizations and churches, was not "trauma-informed." From asking me intimate questions about my sexual past outside of Mark (shame) to asking me to reconcile things I forgot (shame and terror), they did not lead me in the way of healing and instead harmed me in the process. Twenty-two years after my abuse and twelve years after that internal investigation, I can still feel the effects of all those emotions rippling through my body.

Forgetting the details of trauma is a terrifying gift. I have to trust that my body will respond in the way God made it to—to keep me safe in case I do have more memories. I have to remind myself that this is a normal response. Sometimes new memories show up and the trauma response associated with them keeps coming. There is a strange tension in discovering buried information: I'm one step closer to knowing *all* the details of what happened to me, but I'm equally afraid there is more I am forgetting. This is why trauma is such a curse and why we cannot walk through healing alone.

Memories are precious things, usually correlated with positive events, such as a birth, a special family tradition, or time with friends. But memories can also hold terror for abuse survivors and can provoke an extremely and profoundly negative response in survivors that they may not even be aware of. As you engage with a loved one in your life who has been sexually abused, handle those memories with care, and do not force entry into them uninvited. Simply sit and listen, and encourage the survivor in your life to seek not only your friendship and support but that of a properly trained counselor or psychologist as well.

Appendix C

Key Legal Terms

*I*t's important to note that all abuse is evil. All abuse is wrong. All abuse is sinful. Most abuse is criminal to some degree. We need to have clarity on what sexual abuse is by legal, spiritual, and technical definitions.

Every country, and every state within those countries, often has specific laws that define various degrees of sexual abuse. We won't get into every differentiation of the law, but we will learn what the key terms are (listed alphabetically).

I have learned that the vocabulary behind the various acts of sexual abuse can sometimes be misleading one way or another. In my own case, the man who abused me was charged with the criminal act of "sexual assault." To me, the word *assault* conjures up images of a violent rape. My abuse was never violently forced on me. I think it's important to know these variables so that we can communicate clearly without causing any additional harm to survivors or confusing any criminal terminology.

These words and their definitions are not palatable. They shouldn't be. They should cause us to feel sick to our stomachs and evoke a justice-seeking holy rage in us. As you read them, instead of getting lost in the depths of evil and imagining the details of the acts, reflect on the men, women, and children who have endured these horrors. Grieve the innocence that has been stolen from survivors. It's difficult to do, but allow yourself to feel the heaviness of the evil contained in these words. It's important we let the below terms—words that represent acts committed against our fellow men and women—weigh on us.

It is this sorrow that will in turn allow us the room to offer compassion and support.

Terms

Age of consent: This is the age by which the law determines a person is able to reasonably consent to sexual acts. It varies from state to state, and you can usually find it on your state's official government website or by asking a licensed attorney. Acts that are considered sexual usually include the touching of any sexual part of a person's body (including breasts, genital, and anal regions) by any part of another person's body or by an object (e.g., hands touching breasts, sexual intercourse, or kissing any sexual part of a person's body). If a person is under the age of consent, it is considered a crime. The age of consent varies from sixteen to eighteen in most states and countries. But a person's position (teacher, pastor, etc.) supersedes the age of consent. In many states, for example, a teacher cannot have sexual contact with a student under the age of eighteen even if the age of consent is sixteen.

Aggravated sexual assault: Aggravated sexual assault (including all degrees [first, second, third, fourth], rape, forcible touching, and other terms that vary state to state) is the penetration of a sexual organ by another person, or causing another person to penetrate a sexual organ (for instance a female assaulting a male) when the person is under the age of fourteen (in most states), elderly, disabled, or if any weapon is used (including drugs) or any bodily injury or death is intended or occurs. This is a felony.

Consent: Giving permission to have a sexual encounter. Consent cannot be given when a person is under a certain age (see "age of consent") or is impaired due to disability, intoxication, or other impaired mental status.

Date rape: Occurs when a person is on a date or is otherwise physically present with a person (friend, date, boyfriend, girlfriend). It can involve the use of force or drugs. This implies that the people involved are of the age of consent but that consent is not given or is unable to be given (in the instance of being drugged or intoxicated). This is a felony.

Domestic rape: Rape or sexual assault by a spouse or domestic partner. Even when someone is married, they have the right to refuse sex. Within most religions, including Christianity, some people falsely believe it is the husband's spiritual right or authority to have sex even if their spouse says no. In this instance, it is not only sexual abuse, it is spiritual abuse. This is a felony.

Incest: Occurs when a family member engages in a sexual act with another family member (related by blood, adoption, or marriage).

This can happen whether the victim is a minor or is of the age of consent. Blood relatives in most states include parents, siblings, grandparents, aunts, uncles, and first-degree cousins. This law varies from state to state. This is considered a felony.

Indecency with a minor: This is another term for sexual assault or abuse of any kind and varies from state to state in regard to the "degree" one is abused. In most cases, this involves the touching of any sexual organ or body part, such as the breasts, of a minor by another person or object, with the intent of sexual gratification. In many stories having to do with youth pastor/minor relationships, this is generally one of the most common accusations. This is a felony.

Lewd and lascivious behavior: This is another term for sexual assault, abuse, or indecency with a child or minor but also includes any written or electronic communication that suggests a sex act. It can include showing nudity in person or electronically, or urinating or excreting on a person with intent for sexual gratification. In some states this is a felony, and in some states, it is a misdemeanor, depending on the state and situation.

Multiple-perpetrator sexual abuse/assault: Otherwise known as "gang rape," this felony happens when multiple offenders abuse or assault a person, whether it is a minor or someone of consenting age. In these cases, all involved perpetrators are held responsible for the crime.

Pedophile: Someone who is sexually aroused by or who sexually desires a child. Generally, it is understood that this person is attracted to prepubescent children. Being a pedophile is not a crime in and of itself, but acting on one's urges by viewing child pornography, gratifying one's desires using a child or in the presence of a child, or committing a sex act with a child constitutes the offense, which is always a felony.

Pornography: Any image or communication (written, electronic, verbal, printed, and even art) that evokes a sexually gratifying response. Sometimes it is clearly defined by a gratuitous image, but other times pornography can be subtle, depending on the person using it. Someone may view a lingerie catalog with absolutely no sexual gratification or desire, and another person may look at the same catalog with a sexual response and/or gratification. For adults, pornography *can be* subjective. When involving minors in any capacity (viewing, sending, sharing, or showing it to a minor), pornography is not subjective and is illegal.

Predator: Can be an adult or a child who in any way abuses, assaults, or causes harm to another person. The term predator generally defines someone who is a repeat offender.

Prostitution: Performing a sexual act for money or other payment (like drugs). Prostitution is illegal in most places, but in the United States is legal to some extent in Nevada.

Rape: Another term for sexual assault and always includes sexual intercourse. The main differentiating factor between rape and sexual assault in some states is that sexual assault does not always include intercourse.

Sex trafficking: Similar to prostitution but usually implies that another party is selling someone for sexual acts. Child sex trafficking is when someone sells a minor for sexual acts, including online sex or pornography. Victims of trafficking do not consent. This is different from prostitution because prostitution implies consent of the person receiving compensation for sex.

Sexual abuse: A broad term used to describe the abuse of any person by any other person or people for the purpose of sexual gratification or exploitation.

Sexual assault: Generally implies rape but does not always include sexual intercourse, whereas rape always includes sexual intercourse. Usually sexual assault occurs when the victim's body is penetrated by a body part or an object. Most states define penetration as any insertion of a body part into an orifice of another person, no matter how slight that penetration is.

Sexual battery: Usually another legal term for aggravated sexual assault or sexual assault, depending on the state.

Sexual harassment: Generally implies that a person has experienced unwanted sexual attention (touching, communication, stalking, inappropriate staring, forced to look at something sexual) within a place of employment. At minimum, most organizations will write up or dismiss the offender, and sometimes criminal and/or civil charges are pursued.

Sexual misconduct: Many organizations refer to sexual misconduct as any inappropriate sexual behavior. It is a broad term that may or may not carry criminal or civil repercussions. A common policy is a "Zero-Tolerance Sexual Misconduct Policy," which means if a person commits any act of sexual misconduct, they will have ties severed within that organization. Unfortunately, misconduct is often "graded," and those who commit a "lesser" offense (e.g., a person makes a sexual innuendo) may not be subject to such harsh punishments. If you see or hear this term, ask what is meant specifically and what consequences someone will face for even the slightest act of impropriety.

Sexting: Sending sexual content electronically, usually over the phone via social media or text messaging. Sending "nudes" is another example of this. If someone sends or is on the receiving end of child pornography, it is a federal crime. Many states even prosecute minors for sending illicit photos of themselves or other minors.

Sodomy: The act of a penis penetrating the anus. Some laws include digital penetration of the anus or penetration of the anus using objects under the definition of sodomy.

Solicitation of a minor: This is a crime. The offender pursues a sexual act with a minor, whether in person or online (or other electronic means), directly or indirectly (through a parent, caretaker, etc.). This can be for paid sex (child prostitution, child sex trafficking) or for sex acts that are not paid.

Acknowledgments

I extend eternal gratitude to:

Tim, Charlotte, my mom, dad, brother, and grandma: Thank you is not enough for the sacrifices you have made through the years, especially the last year, in caring for my family and me. You have carried more weight than you needed to, which has lifted this burden off my shoulders so I can heal.

My friends in person and online: You have been Jesus in flesh and blood and pixels and emails. Your prayers and grace as I wrestle through this situation and with my faith has encouraged me beyond anything I could ever ask.

Sarah Smith and Robert Downen and the other journalists and writers who keep this issue in the forefront of society's mind: In creating and holding a trustworthy space for my story and many others, you have brought this subject to the front of the church—something church leaders should have been doing from the beginning. You set the world on fire for survivors and brought the reckoning.

Detective Charles Cisneros and Assistant District Attorney William Knight: You have seen me at my most vulnerable, listened to unspeakable details with compassion and grace, and have taken every hard step for justice to be done on my behalf. Thank you for believing me and fighting for truth.

My psychiatric and medical professionals whom I will not name because I believe in HIPAA and PHI: Thank you for keeping me talking and using the appropriate chemicals when necessary so that I can function despite the traumatizing effects of sexual abuse. You are a necessary part of my healing now and in the future.

Candice and the Casita: Your space gave me space to write this and rest. Your hospitality is a gift to many, and I'm grateful to you for opening your home and heart to me.

To the teams at Lifeway and Zondervan: Your belief in me, my story, my hope, and your skill of mastering these words with a red pen have brought a tangible redemption of my story as it (hopefully) helps others.

All survivors: Regardless of whether your story has been spoken out loud or quietly in your own heart, you are brave and loved and not alone. You did nothing to deserve what you have endured, and I pray healing for you on this earth as much as can be had.

I extend eternal urging to:

Those who have done the harm: I cannot thank you, but I can and I do pray for you. As long as you have breath, you also have hope. I urge you to confess, repent, reconcile, and restore what damage you have done. We will carry on regardless, but I believe healing comes with being held to account for your actions and, in some cases, your crime. You have the choice to do everything in your power to make things right. Please do it.

Please do it.

Notes

PREFACE

1. Robert Downen, Sarah Smith, John Tedesco, and Lise Olsen, "Abuse of Faith," Parts 1-6, *Houston Chronicle*, February–June 2019, https://www.houstonchronicle.com/local/investigations /abuse-of-faith/.

2. "Southern Baptists Face Calls for Criminal Probe into Sexual Abuse Report," NPR's Morning Edition. February 13, 2019, Host: Rachel Martin, https://www.npr.org/2019/02/13 /694174991/southern-baptists-face-calls-for-criminal -probe-into-sexual-abuse-report.

CHAPTER 1: MY STORY OF CHILDHOOD CLERGY SEXUAL ABUSE

1. "Molested by a Priest: Confronting a Child Molester," *The Oprah Winfrey Show*, June 13, 2005.

CHAPTER 2: THE DIFFERENT TYPES OF ABUSE

1. "Sexual Assault of Young Children as Reported to Law Enforcement: Victim, Incident, and Offender Characteristics," Bureau of Justice Statistics, https://www.bjs.gov/content/pub /pdf/saycrle.pdf.

2. Child Sexual Abuse Statistics, The National Center for Victims of Crime, http://victimsofcrime.org/media/reporting-on-child -sexual-abuse/child-sexual-abuse-statistics.

3. Transactional Reference Access Clearing House, https://trac.syr .edu/laws/18/18USC02423.html.

4. Unless otherwise cited, these are from "Useful Definitions for Reporting on Child Sexual Abuse," The National Center for Victims of Crime, http://victimsofcrime.org/media/reporting-on -child-sexual-abuse/useful-definitions.

5. Roxanne Dryden-Edwards, "Child Abuse," https://www. medicinenet.com/child_abuse_facts/article.htm#what_are _symptoms_and_signs_of_child_abuse.

6. "What Is Domestic Violence?" The National Domestic Abuse Hotline, https://www.thehotline.org/is-this-abuse/abuse -defined/.

CHAPTER 3: WHO ARE THE PERPETRATORS?

1. Anna Salter, *Predators: Pedophiles, Rapists, and Other Sex Offenders* (New York: Basic, 2003).

2. "Children and Teens: Statistics," RAIN, https://www.rainn.org /statistics/children-and-teens.

3. "Statistics on Perpetrators of Childhood Sexual Abuse," The National Center for Victims of Crime, http://victimsofcrime .org/media/reporting-on-child-sexual-abuse/ statistics-on-perpetrators-of-csa.

4. "Diagnostic and Statistical Manual of Mental Disorders, fourth ed, (Washington, DC: American Psychiatric Association, 2000).

5. Conte, Wolf and Smith. 1989 [need more info]. Quoted in Anna Salter, *Predators: Pedophiles, Rapists, and Other Sex Offenders* (New York: Basic, 2003), need page number.

6. Salter, *Predators*, need page number.

7. Ibid.

8. Ibid.

9. Ibid.

10. Ibid.
11. RAINN: The Criminal Justice System Statistics. https://www
    .rainn.org/statistics/criminal-justice-system.

CHAPTER 4: SURVIVORS AND VICTIMS

 1. Anne Marie Miller, *5 Things Every Parent Needs to Know about
    Their Kids and Sex* (Grand Rapids: Baker, 2016), need page
    number.
 2. Bessel Van der Kolk, *The Body Keeps the Score: Brain, Mind, and
    Body in the Healing of Trauma* (New York: Viking, 2014).
 3. Ibid.
 4. The first three responses come from L. Hamilton, "Fight, Flight
    or Freeze: Implications of the Passive Fear Response for Anxiety
    and Depression," *Phobia Practice and Research Journal*, 1989,
    2(1):17–27. The fourth response, *fawn*, comes from Pete Walker,
    MA, MFT's article, "Codependency, Trauma, and the Fawn
    Response," *The East Bay Therapist*, Jan/Feb 2003.

CHAPTER 5: UNDERSTANDING THE ROLE OF SUPPORTERS

 1. Anne Marie Miller, *Lean on Me: Finding Intentional,
    Vulnerable, and Consistent Community* (Nashville: Thomas
    Nelson, 2014).
 2. "Types of Mental Health Professionals," National Alliance
    on Mental Illness, April 2019, https://www.nami.org
    /Learn-More/Treatment/Types-of-Mental-Health-
    Professionals.
 3. S. Acharya and S. Shukla, "Mirror Neurons: Enigma
    of the Metaphysical Modular Brain," *Journal of Natural
    Science, Biology and Medicine*, 3, no. 2 (2012):118–124.
    doi:10.4103/0976–9668.101878

CHAPTER 6: HELPING SURVIVORS: A PRACTICAL GUIDE

 1. Definition of *compassion*, Online Etymology Dictionary, https://
    www.etymonline.com/word/compassion.

CHAPTER 7: PREVENTING, RECOGNIZING, AND RESPONDING TO CHILDHOOD SEXUAL ABUSE

1. "Statistics on Children and Teens," RAINN, https://www.rainn.org/statistics/children-and-teens.
2. "Instruments of Hope and Healing: Safeguarding Children and Young People," Conference of Major Superiors of Men, 2016, http://image.jesuits.org/UCSPROV/media/Instruments_Hope_Healing.pdf.
3. "5 Steps to Protecting Our Children," Darkness to Light, 2017, https://www.d2l.org/wp-content/uploads/2017/01/5-Steps-to-Protecting-Our-Kids-2017.pdf.
4. "Education," Darkness to Light, https://www.d2l.org/education/.
5. "Tip Sheet: Warning Signs of Possible Sexual Abuse in a Child's Behavior," Stop It Now! https://www.stopitnow.org/ohc-content/tip-sheet-7.
6. "Behaviors to Watch Out for When Adults are with Children," Stop It Now!, https://www.stopitnow.org/ohc-content/behaviors-to-watch-out-for-when-adults-are-with-children.
7. P. Valdesolo and D. DeSteno, "Moral Hypocrisy: Social Groups and the Flexibility of Virtue," *Psychological Science*, 18, no. 8 (2007): 689–690. https://doi.org/10.1111/j.1467-9280.2007.01961.x.
8. Rachel Held Evans, "No More Silence: An Interview with Boz Tchividjian of G.R.A.C.E," March 18, 2013, https://rachelheldevans.com/blog/abuse-boz-tchividjian.

CONCLUSION

1. Diane Langberg, *Counseling Survivors of Sexual Abuse* (Maitland, FL: Xulon, 2003), 69.
2. Ibid, 134.

APPENDIX A: WHAT IS TRAUMA?

1. "DSM-5 Criteria for PTSD," Brainline, https://www.brainline.org/article/dsm-5-criteria-ptsd.

2. "Coping with Traumatic Events," February 2017, National Institute of Mental Health, https://www.nimh.nih.gov/health /topics/coping-with-traumatic-events/index.shtml.

3. Jennie G. Noll, Meg H. Zeller, Penelope K. Trickett, Frank W. Putnam, "Victims of Childhood Sexual Abuse: A Prospective Study," *Pediatrics*, 120, no. 1, (Jul 2007): e61–e67; DOI: 10.1542/peds.2006-3058

4. J. E. Sherin and C. B. Nemeroff, "Post-Traumatic Stress Disorder: The Neurobiological Impact of Psychological Trauma," *Dialogues in Clinical Neuroscience*, 13, no. 3 (2011): 263–278.

5. Olga Kahzan, "The Second Assault," December 15, 2015, *The Atlantic*, https://www.theatlantic.com/health/archive/2015/12 /sexual-abuse-victims-obesity/420186/.

6. "Adult Manifestations of Childhood Sexual Abuse," August 2011, Committee Opinion No. 498, American College of Obstetricians and Gynecologists, 118:392–95.

7. Ibid.

8. L. S. Bensley, J. Van Eenwyk, K. W. Simmons, "Self-Reported Childhood Sexual and Physical Abuse and Adult Hiv-Risk Behaviors and Heavy Drinking," *American Journal of Preventative Medicine*, 18, no. 2 (Feb 2000): 151–58.

9. D. A. Baram and R. Basson, "Sexuality, Sexual Dysfunction, and Sexual Assault" in J. S. Berek, ed. *Berek & Novak's Gynecology, 14th ed.* (Philadelphia: Lippincott, Williams & Wilkins, 2007), 313–49.

10. P. P. Rieker and E. H. Carmen, "The Victim-To-Patient Process: The Disconfirmation and Transformation of Abuse," *American Journal of Orthopsychiatry* 56 (1986): 360–70.

APPENDIX B: UNDERSTANDING TRAUMATIC MEMORY

1. Dr. Elizabeth Loftus and Katherine Ketcham, *The Myth of Repressed Memory: False Memories and Allegations of Sexual Abuse, 1st ed.* (New York: St. Martin's, 1994), 90.

2. Shari R. Berkowitz et. al., "Pluto Behaving Badly: False Beliefs and Their Consequences," *American Journal of Psychology* 121, no. 4 (Winter 2008), https://webfiles.uci.edu/eloftus/Berkowitz _Pluto_AJP08.pdf.

3. S. D. Neill, "The Reference Process and Certain Types of Memory: Semantic, Episodic, and Schematic," *Reference Quarterly* 23 (1984): 417–23.

4. Krishnagopal Dharani, "Memory" in The Biology of Thought: *A Neural Mechanism in the Generation of Thought—A New Molecular Model* (London: Academic, 2015), https://www.sciencedirect .com/topics/neuroscience/implicit-memory.

5. Megan E. Giroux et al., "Reconstructing the Past," in Philippe Tortell et al., *Memory* (Vancouver: Peter Wall Institute for Advanced Studies, 2018), 151.

6. Ibid.